MW01644530

LAUGHTER ON MY PATH

An Educator's Funny and Compelling Encounters with People, Problems, and Pets

Ann Lowrance Allman, Ed.D.

WestBow Press books may be ordered through booksellers or by contacting:

WestBow Press
A Division of Thomas Nelson & Zondervan
1663 Liberty Drive
Bloomington, IN 47403
www.westbowpress.com
1 (866) 928-1240

ISBN: 978-1-4908-2960-9 (sc)
ISBN: 978-1-4908-2962-3 (hc)
ISBN: 978-1-4908-2961-6 (e)

Library of Congress Control Number: 2014904473

Printed in the United States of America.

WestBow Press rev. date: 04/28/2014

Acknowledgements

To Dr. Jack Allman, my wonderful husband and best friend, I owe my deepest thanks for his many funny stories and for helping me toward the book's completion. Millie Stover, my long-term friend and colleague, took out her English teacher red pen to that awful first manuscript. Educator Barbara Odneal, who collaborated with me in writing for our school newspapers, provided hoorahs and questions and gently reminded me about some excess bathroom humor, which I took out. Brenda Plagmann from the greenhouse days added some more stories.

Author-colleague Robin Montz found chapters without good transitions and noticed I had misspelled the word tyrannosauruses. Writer-artist Lee Mitchell helped tell on my husband's classmates and noticed where I had left literary holes. My classmate Dr. Bill Bunker helped with grammar and spelling, and my neighbors, Bea Nodler, Marvin and Freda Smith, Rosemary Lehar, and Ned Sloan responded to the book from a general public perspective, with Bea and Rosemary helping to search for more errors.

Thanks to authors Jo Pearcy and Charlie Nodler, who wrote up their thoughts about the book, and to Dr. Bill Chambliss and writer Vince Williams, who helped me agonize over title changes. Retired Crowder College librarian, Barb Schade, cleaned up some things the rest of us had missed. My youngest son, Dennis Hamilton, encouraged me to express more of my feelings. And thanks to those who gave permission to use their stories and their names and who tattled on themselves even further.

A big thank-you also goes to Jessica Cecilla, Brittany Bingle, Katie Diamond, Mason Rose, and to all the folks at Westbow Press, who helped me during the publication process.

My life has been enriched by all the funny people and animals in my life, who were just themselves and who have made this world a happier place.

Dedication

To my husband, Dr. Jack Allman, who first knew me
when I did not know where I was going in the school business.
He turned my first job as an administrator into my dream job,
yet knew I had a counselor heart as well.

And to my parents, Dr. Edward and Elizabeth Lowrance,
who taught me never to be afraid to reach for
the wonderfully impossible or unusual.

Preface

One day in eighth grade, a sweet, cheerful classmate came up to me and said, "You're funny!"

"I am?"

"Yeah, and you ought to be writing our class column in the school newspaper so we can all get some laughs." By then, I was really surprised and complimented.

Her comments made me think about my good Christian parents. I knew my mother was full of mischief, and my straight-laced father could sum up a funny story in one sentence. However, I'd been too busy playing with my pet lizard and grackle to focus on much of anything else, except for having to face some reluctant puberty and learning how to play my clarinet without making it squeak.

Suddenly, a light turned on. I grabbed up my best friend, Barbara, and we started sitting in the grass, consumed with an almost terminal case of the sillies, and began writing for the newspaper - even enlisting others to tell on our peers.

That was just the beginning. Soon I asked myself, why not choose to make a difference in people's lives by trying to make them laugh over real life? In fact, why couldn't I actually *decide* to be a happy person and stick with it? For a start, I began reading Mother's funny annual Christmas letters that she wrote to family and friends and used some of the ideas in them to write essays for English class. Then I began saving her letters, wondering what I might do with them.

Now fast-forward to the day, at age 29, when the Lord had me by the nap of the neck and propelled me into Joplin High School to become dean of girls, with nothing but my expired, temporary Spanish teaching certificate for credentials. That's when the real challenge began, as they had forgotten to tell me I was also to be the girls' disciplinarian and school nurse. Among all those great kids, the trouble-makers were already lying in wait with their lists. However, I was determined to outsmart them and to keep a smile on my face. After just a few months of that, people started telling me I should write a book. So I took a lot of notes.

By the time I finally retired as a college counselor, the mound of book-promoters had grown too high, and some of my older advisees started heckling, asking if I were going to get the book done before they died. So now you can read about the whole, rollicking adventure, which is pretty well unvarnished and with some of the rougher spots sanded down a bit.

CONTENTS

PART I

PART II

PART III

PART I

Chapter 1

HANGING FROM THE FAMILY TREE

My mother acted like she had a master's degree in methods for outsmarting first graders, in spite of what her diploma said. Father had a Ph.D. in something between biology and medicine, and toyed with cadavers, embryos, and skeletons. Whatever was to become of me, I figured I could blame on the family genes. Years later my colleagues said all this explained a lot of things, especially after I told them I played with bugs and rodents when I was a child.

I meandered through grade school in the forties and junior high in the early fifties thinking I might become a nurse like many of the other girls my age did. By the time I graduated from high school, I was still the Queen of Indecision. I had experienced an illustrious musical career for a teenager, but didn't want a life of married clarinet players asking me for dates on the road. My senior year I had been all-too-moved at church camp to pledge my life to full-time Christian service and join missionary forces. I loved the Lord; however, at seventeen, I was having a hard time dealing with distorted thoughts of fleas in my cot and aborigines with bones through their noses hovering over me. An affordable religious education school was nowhere in sight anyway.

Halfway domesticated, I figured a home economics major could at least show me how to cook and sew better, plus a few other things. I could teach students how to make pajamas without sewing the legs together like I did once in tenth grade. But when I found out how much chemistry I would have to take, I counted my chemistry scars and threw that out.

I sped off to junior college full of my mother Elizabeth's admonitions that a girl without a college education would never amount to anything. Was I destined to become a teacher like my parents? As entertaining as they were, I had experienced enough of Mother's first grade stories. When someone cheated at the blackboard, she claimed "blackboard disease" was spreading. If she couldn't catch a boy copying off a girl beside him, she waited until he also copied her name. If someone missed the toilet in her bathroom and the next guy didn't report it, that next guy had to clean it up.

On the other hand, was I to be like my father, Edward, finishing off students in medical school? He had already told me how to hang a cadaver using ice tongs in his ears so he could be lowered into a vat of formaldehyde. I pored over medical student yearbooks, one shamelessly sporting a picture of a dirigible-size tank labeled, "Twenty-Four Hour Urine Sample." I had studied Father's two-headed pig embryo in a jar and a baby that was supposed to be twins in another one. It had three eyes, half a brain, and six fingers and toes on each extremity. I had listened to Father's story about being the last person in the department to get a leg found in a sewer so he could help identify it by measuring the bones.

At least I decided I was not going to be one of Father's students and become a nurse. No way was I was going to do guts, blood, bones, or pus. I did read a whole book on obstetrics for nurses some years later so I could shuck out my babies like peas.

Perhaps Mother thought she could inspire me into a career choice by relentlessly trying to get me interested in my heritage. She had already stomped through endless cemeteries wearing her rain boots, taking pictures of tombstones speckled with bird droppings and dead grass blades so she could tell stories about the people lying under them. Among all of her minister, doctor, and musical relatives, she was proud she had found at least one horse thief, but was incensed when someone tried to convince her that Napoleon was part of our family tree. I wasn't quite sure where all this was going, but something told me I should pay attention in case there was a genetic or environmental trap hiding somewhere.

Part of my problem with career indecision was that I was also a victim of too much family versatility, meaning there wasn't much my parents were afraid to tackle. In addition to their careers, between the two of them they could play musical instruments, draw, sew, write scientific papers, speak a foreign language, do carpentry work with impeccable precision, identify animals and insects that bit people and each other, collect weird specimens and remember all their names, think of pranks to pull on the neighbors, raise vegetables and chickens, fix machinery without leaving out some of the parts, and work algebraic equations with two unknowns. Amid all that, my visions of a career path were still dim and I was looking for focus.

My father's parents were a different sort. Their lives had been simple. By the time I was five, I only remembered being around Grandma Edith Lowrance a few times before she lost her mind. Father showed her all the exercises she could do to overcome most of the crippling from her stroke, but sadly, at age sixty-eight or so, she claimed she was too old to bother. After the stroke, my younger sister, Janet, and I kept a suspicious eye on her. She could make Cream of Wheat and fry eggs for breakfast without mishap, even with only one usable hand. When it came to toast, she waited until the smoke rolled out of the toaster before dropping the sides down and loudly proclaimed, "Burnt toast!" Supper was canned green beans and poached hamburgers boiled over a wood stove. Grandpa Sam, the quiet bookkeeper, was known to pour out a lot of funny one-liners about people, but he knew better during this time in his life than to open his mouth about what he had to put in it.

Being an avid animal lover, the thing I looked forward to the most when we went to visit them was their bird. Before we were born, Grandpa inherited Polly, Mother's lame-winged, semi-retarded, double yellow-headed parrot that was purchased for her when she was fourteen. She and Father were not allowed to keep him in their apartment after they got married. Grandpa was euphoric.

To him, it was a perfect match. The bird was full of the devil, which didn't please Grandma a whole lot, especially since he liked to bite strange women. Grandpa built him a four-rung standing perch so he could be free of his cage during the day. Eventually Polly chewed the top rung in half, causing him to lean sideways. Later Grandpa put metal stripping down the sides to make it difficult for him to climb down and bite the toes of a neighbor lady whom he despised. She was always loudly crooning, "Here birdy, birdy!" in his face, which irritated him to the core. However, when the lady was out of earshot, Grandpa would whisper in the bird's ear, "Sic her."

Since he couldn't fly, Polly was given free reign of the back yard cherry tree. He screamed at the neighbors until they finally came over and complained. Grandpa said, "You can climb up there and kill him if you want to."

Getting Polly to come back in every night was a ritual. He would stall Grandpa off with a few arias from some bird opera he knew. Then he would climb down the tree and let Grandpa pick him up. He would carry the bird into the house on his shoulder, letting him pick his nose and groom his eyebrows and ear hairs on the way in.

Polly ate what Grandpa did except for sunflower seeds. The bird thought fried eggs and soda crackers soaked in coffee for breakfast were the cat's meow and would sing "A 'racker," until he got his. After he was done, Polly would climb down to the bottom of his cage and bite off a piece of newspaper to clean his beak. Then he would sharpen it on the rungs of his cage to get ready for the neighbor lady.

Mother's father, Walter Patton the banker, was unique. He was undaunted by challenges, and between him and Mother, there didn't seem to be anybody or anything they couldn't outfox, including under the hood of the family Model T Ford. It didn't bother her that she was also treated as if she were her father's oldest son, nor was he in any way concerned about what anyone thought about him teaching her how to knit and make doll clothes.

Several years after Grandfather died at forty-eight from cancer, Mother opened a letter from her mother, Mabel. Suddenly she sat down hard on the front porch, bellowing, "Well! Mama has just eloped with Uncle Will!" She muttered things under her breath for an hour, furious that her mother had neither clued her in nor invited her to the wedding. I thought that was all pretty neat, but Mother still wanted to hiss about it some more. Who cared if he was now Grandma's husband and brother-in-law, Mother's stepfather and uncle, and my grandpa and great-uncle?

What Mother hadn't found out yet, was that a couple of years before marrying Grandma, Uncle Will's own wife, Maude, was found to be dying from cancer. As Maude's end drew closer, he told Grandma that a year after Maude died, he wanted to marry her so she would always have someone to take care of her. Soon after they were married, I saw him in our kitchen, holding his tearful new wife close to him and reaffirming his promise. That was just too sweet, and for a brief moment, I told my six-year-old self that if she ever left him, I'd marry him myself.

Our new Patton grandpa was a childless master carpenter, thrilled to inherit grandchildren. Unlike our grandpa Lowrance, who, with a twinkle in his eye, would shake our hands after not seeing us for a year, Grandpa Patton was a warm, slobbery, kiss-on-the-lips hugger. I was elated when I had the chance to live with them in San Jose for three months. I had experienced a serious bout with pneumonia four years earlier, and Mother thought my health might improve by sniffing some good California air.

My soft-spoken grandma immediately hauled me off to church with her to help with the World War II effort, where I helped cut out slippers for the women to sew together for the soldiers. The rest of the time, I stayed in the church kitchen and plucked chickens that had been plunged into boiling cauldrons. I never could figure out what stinky plucked chickens had to do with the war effort.

Sunday mornings were another matter. Grandma was no longer soft-spoken and had a beautiful, loud voice, which almost blew out the candles during church services. It wasn't enhanced by her singing a fourth-note off key and a half-beat behind. The congregation had gotten used to her, but I had relative pitch, and her singing made my teeth itch.

Grandpa spent his spare time making us pretty things out of wood, like jewelry boxes and lamps, including lamps out of abalone shells. One day he got possessed with himself and decided to make a whole boat destined to be christened "The Mabel." It would have been a fine piece of work, had he not decided to build a square cabin over it. Sure enough, the first time he launched it, it began heaving in the wind like a dog trying to throw up a dead bird. Mother suggested they put on hip boots and do some less risky clam hunting instead.

By the time I was seven or eight, he had built Grandma a beautiful home and settled down into grafting fruit trees. It wasn't a pretty sight, but it did keep Grandpa off the streets. That was a worry all by itself, as he drove with no sense of reason. He had a philosophy about stop signs. He would do his duty and stop and then he would gun it. He said if there were any idiots in his way, they'd have to look out for themselves.

It was always a treat to go to their house, where my sister, Janet, and I would gobble up Grandma's homemade rolls, killer apple pies, and tasty vegetables. Surprisingly, Mother never did learn much about cooking from her. After giving up on homemade apple pies, Mother finally managed to make cinnamon rolls, which she would sometimes forget about while they were rising in the cupboard. They would crawl out the door and be halfway to the sink before she would discover them.

Unfortunately, Grandpa had horrible cravings for Grandma's wonderful, fried, and very fat bacon. Three hours later, he would be writhing in pain on the couch, bloated like an old dirigible. I never could figure out how he could pass so much gas without a sound.

I thought a lot about my grandparents and what they were doing with their lives. I knew when I grew up, I wouldn't give a hoot about taking care of someone else's money like my grandfathers did. However, watching Grandma Patton cook was fun, except for that fried fat business and all the chicken plucking. Maybe I could learn to be a cook.

Polly and Mother's sister Ruth 1927

Chapter 2

THE PRUDES IN SIN CITY

Father, the wonderful, benevolent, only-child nerd seemed to know everything there was to learn about biology, but had absolutely no skills whatsoever for chasing women. He was just too cerebral and straight-laced. It wasn't until I was in the upper grades, that my less naïve mother even told me how she and Father had met. When he first saw her at church in Salt Lake City in 1929, he liked her looks and met with her after the service. As far as we knew, she seemed to be the only woman he ever went after. Pretty soon they had to figure out cheap dates, as Father didn't know how to drive because Grandpa and Grandma could never afford a car. Mother took up a little of that slack, as she at least had a Model T Ford named Ichabod, which ran when it got good and ready. She secretly taught him to drive later, when no one was looking.

In those days, two prudish people necking in a car where everyone could see in was obviously out of the question, so they figured they could pack a couple of lunches and go hunting for lizards in the Wasatch mountains instead. Then they put the lizards in their empty lunch sacks and headed for the movies. The lizards took a dim view of the whole thing and wanted out and began scratching inside the sacks loudly enough to disturb the entire theater. That didn't keep Mother and Father from several repeat performances, but in different movie houses, so they wouldn't get thrown out.

Their almost six-year engagement ended in 1935, when they felt they had to rush into marriage before Mother's father died. By that time, Father was in the throes of graduate school at Stanford University, trying to drum up something for his doctoral dissertation. Lizards in sacks had obviously taken a quantum leap away from his attentions. He was now working on the topic, "Determination of Polarity in Eggs of Fucus Furcatus by Temperature Gradients." Mother thought that sounded too obscene to explain to polite company, so she came up with a bogus translation that people could understand called, "The Effect of Temperature on Seaweed Eggs." She helped him for hours, running back and forth between rooms in their house, checking thermometers. At least it helped Father get his doctorate so he could finally get Mother pregnant with me instead of spending all of his time fertilizing seaweed eggs.

He got his first job as a biology teacher at the University of Nevada in Reno. We lived so close to campus, that on most days, Father walked to work, often taking me with him. Father's lab was across from a glass display case full of stuffed, totally life-like, white pelicans. I knew I wasn't supposed to touch anything, but I was dying for him to let them out so I could play with them.

After Father explained the predicament of pickled pelicans, he brought me some departmental specimen earwigs to play with. Father didn't let me get too interested in them, or the pincers on their rear ends, before he told me we had some of the insect's merciless relatives in our yard, eating the foliage in the victory garden. The object lesson was to learn to carefully handle insects so I could help him rid the property of them later to the tune of a nickel a dozen reward and a lot of toilet flushing. Those were pretty good wages for a little girl.

Sometimes as we were walking along, I'd ask Father if I should step on a certain bug. He'd say, "He didn't do anything to you, did he?"

Finally I asked him, "How can I tell if a bug is going to bite?"

"Bring it to me and I'll tell you."

Now something was wrong with this picture. Was I to risk picking up some evil-eyed, stingy-thing with furry horns over his eyes, just to find out whether or not it was going to bite? Father quickly discovered the error of his ways and got me a mayonnaise jar with holes punched in the lid.

Sometimes on weekends, we went out into the desert to catch "hornytoads," a name I had to eventually abandon. Horned toads could run pretty fast, but sun-baked, they were easy to catch. They weren't prone to domestication, so we just caught them for the heck of it, turned them loose, and went home. As we left, we skirted the rocks and rattlesnake hiding places as if lepers lived there, knowing this was no match for the mayonnaise jar.

There wasn't much that turned Mother's stomach, but the day Father brought home a human brain before supper, she kept it a secret that she was about to lose it. It came in a rectangular-shaped, covered, white porcelain pan. With great fanfare, Father placed it on the kitchen table, separating our dinner plates with it as if it were some elegant table centerpiece. Flicking his wrists, he uncovered it, brought out his probe, and gently stuck it deeply down into the brain's lobes. That even brought my pet salamander out of his mud house to look.

Father explained that this was the brain of some professor and that the deeper the lobes in a brain, the smarter the person was. I was fascinated, oblivious to the hour and to the hamburgers poaching behind me. I wondered for some time afterwards how Father knew that was a professor, who had killed him, and what they had done with the rest of the body.

Where Father was the master of facts, especially medical ones, Mother was the master of logic. When it was time for me to walk one block to the grocery store by myself, there was no question about what some dead animal in the street had failed to do before he crossed it. She had a way of using logic to trick me, as well as her students later, into believing there wasn't much one couldn't do, or even figure out, after hearing the words "Can you think of any good reason why you can't.....?" If there were no good reason, it was assumed we could do it.

Soon it was time for me to start first grade. By the middle of the year, I had become quite a blabbermouth, and my teacher finally had enough of me and banished me to the coat room for an hour. It was the first and only time I was ever punished at school. I thought it grossly unfair, compared to the little villains that had been sent there before. So I sat there in tears for awhile. I was not a vengeful child, but something came over me. I picked my nose and wiped it on the wall and covered it with a coat. I stifled laughter and walked out, feeling a whole lot better.

Reno was something Father never really got used to, in spite of all its good qualities. For a man who thought lipstick and dyed hair were sinful, the likes of some Reno women, with lipstick running up to their noses and cowboy hats covering their bleached blonde hair, insulted him.

Gambling houses right around the corner from the church blew his mind. Equally awful, his home address was in the U.S. divorce capitol. No wonder his mother had a stroke.

Surprisingly, it was safe for children to walk up and down Virginia Street alone where many of the casinos were, as long as you could dodge drunks. I would occasionally peek through a casino window, but I could never go into one because I was under age. Once I saw a lady in a fur coat standing next to one in rags, both playing the slot machines. On a side street, I saw a man throwing baby clothes out of his car and slinging them into the fast-moving water in the gutter, blaspheming with each gesture. A woman was crying inside the car.

It irritated Father that the casinos would provide so much for the town. The Fourth of July was celebrated each year for a whole month, culminating with a spectacular fireworks display provided for by some of the gambling houses. Citizens were required to wear bandanas around their necks during this time, or be put in the "hoosegow," a traveling jail that displayed you behind bars to the whole citizenry. You had to pay a fine to get out. Mother, who had become the Methodist Church secretary, was secretly hoping the minister would forget to wear his so she could get a picture of him behind bars.

He wasn't the only minister. With so many divorces, the church also had to hire a marrying minister. I hung around church a lot in the summer, often roped into being a witness to spur of the moment weddings, with no one there but the bride and groom. I don't know how many marriage documents I signed, barely able to print.

Rumor had it that it was customary for a divorcee to throw her old wedding rings into the Truckee River before re-marrying. The river ran in front of the church, but the only thing I ever got out of it was a smelly, writhing two pound fish.

Besides being church secretary, Mother kept up with her clarinet playing that she had started in her high school days. She joined the Reno city band that played in local parades. They almost always put the band behind a group of horses, which thoroughly disgusted her. One day she complained, "You have to have three eyes to march in that band. One to watch the music, one to stay in line, and one to watch for horse piles."

Music wasn't Mother's only passion. She had started taking pictures at age fourteen, and it had become her number one hobby. She and Father managed to scrape up enough money to set up a darkroom in the basement. To make some extra money, she started up a little business and took pictures of some of her friends. One day she announced she was going to give that up and just take pictures of children and dogs because they didn't gripe about their wrinkles when they got their pictures back.

There were perceived dangers during these war years too. Living so close to California and the side of the United States closest to Japan, we were constantly warned never to pick up strange objects found in the yard in case they were explosives. I would check the skies for enemy planes, wondering how the gliders being pulled along by C-47s were going to land without crashing. Worse yet, I didn't know what enemy planes were supposed to look like. Anyway, what was I supposed to do if I saw one? There was no 911, and everyone was on a party line.

Mother finally got sick of the party line. Finally she plugged in Father's electric shaver next to the phone and turned it up to roar. When the parties finally hung up due to telephone interference, she made her call.

Father was always on the alert for a better paying job as well as wanting to put his medical school training to better use. He was soon able to take the place of a University of Kansas at Lawrence medical school professor, who wanted to take a two year leave of absence. There was no money to bring the family, so we stayed in Reno the first year, while he stayed rent free in the professor's house close to campus, until he could build up enough funds to bring us there.

Soon after the family arrived in 1945, Father introduced me to my first cadaver. I certainly didn't expect him to be dark brown and wearing a black mustache. I asked Father where all the bodies had come from. He told me some people wanted to donate their bodies to science after they died. Some were bodies of old winos nobody claimed. Once a couple got all huffy about a cadaver, claiming it was their Uncle Ed, and wanted to sue the University for having it illegally. Father caught up with them when they produced Uncle Ed's false teeth for "proof," but the cadaver still had his own.

We had to change churches when we moved to Lawrence because there wasn't a Methodist Church there. So we went to the Christian Church, which I found out had been Mother and Father's original denomination of choice. I asked Mother why we never went to the Christian Church in Reno, and she said it was because they always had a fight going. The Lawrence church was such a wonderful place to be that I decided to make my confession of faith there and be baptized. Besides, in my child's mind, the thought of being immersed in Christ's love meant so much more than being sprinkled by a Methodist minister who seemed to be taking short cuts so he could get home to dinner on time. You could tell I needed to mature in my faith.

When we returned to our home in Reno in the summer of 1946, I needed to change my church membership, but I had to take classes before the Methodists would let me do it. I thought that was a bit unnecessary, since I obviously felt a little more holy because of the immersion thing. In the meantime, it was nice to be home again, where I could look up at the Hosanna Arch in the front of the sanctuary. The faces of Janet and me had been sculpted there, along with the faces of all of the other little children ranging from ages two to five, who were going to church there the day a sculptress came to town. She told the church she could do all of our faces if someone in the congregation would take our pictures for her. Mother offered to do it, and before long, we found out what a priceless artistic gift the lady had.

In 2003, while I was visiting in Reno, I went back to the church one Sunday morning and looked up at that same Hosanna Arch over the front stained glass window and searched again for Janet's and my faces. When I returned home, I told about my wonderful trip and quipped to our Sunday morning Disciples of Christ Christian Church congregation that my sister and I had been up there scaring the Methodists for sixty years.

Reno United Methodist Church Hosannah Arch

Chapter 3

DANCING TO PUBERTY'S TUNE AND SO MANY HORNS TO HONK

Our year in Kansas wasn't anything compared to what we experienced after our move from Reno to Vermillion, South Dakota, in 1949, headed toward Father's first real job of his own as a medical school professor. We found faculty housing trailer-like, with splits between the walls and the ceiling so you could see out. When it rained, our 1936 Ford sank into mud up to its tailbone. Mud seemed like some kind of a trap to snare children and old cars and cause Father to say his worst swear words, which were *"Oh, rats!"*

Grade school would sometimes be called off on a moment's notice because of an impending blizzard, and we would have to race home before it hit. The first time one did, the snow covered up the back of our house and left the front side bare. Some fellow on the other side of town dug a two-story tunnel on the front side of his, which I figured was showing off a bit since his front door was only seven feet high.

South Dakota was noted for its fine music program, and right away I had a chance to learn a musical instrument. Since we couldn't afford a new one, I had a choice of Mother's old metal clarinet resembling a piece of shot-at plumbing, Father's trumpet that made his face turn red and his nose run, and an old violin with some strings hanging from it in all directions. I picked the clarinet, and Janet picked the trumpet, and soon the neighbors knew to start quivering.

Mother realized if we were to have any kind of a family band, we were one instrument short. She decided I needed a new clarinet so she could use her old one and try to make it sound like a flute. She scraped money together for the cheapest one Sears and Roebuck had and ordered it. It didn't matter if the holes in it were too big for my fingers. I made do out of sheer gratitude.

Right away some rickety music stands popped up out of an old trunk, and with that menacing sight, Father got lost. He hoped Janet wouldn't want to change her mind and play the violin instead of his trumpet, as Mother might try to convince him to play it when she started herding us outside to serenade the neighbors. Having to perform in front of the neighbors was pretty embarrassing, but at least my life was pointing in some sort of direction by learning how to play something.

However, nothing was as embarrassing as sixth grade and the onset of puberty. I'd been warned in a book about such antics, but wasn't prepared for the agony of having only one boob. You'd think with two sides to my body, there could have been some kind of justice, but there was no mercy whatsoever for about half a year.

I got real nosy about the other sixth grade girls and tried to spy on them in gym class, using slits for eyes. One lucky girl was fully developed, and if she hadn't been the smartest girl in class, I would have sworn she got her head start by being held back a year. They didn't make clothes for lopsided people, so I had to do the best I could with little wads of tissue on the left side, that somehow found their way to my navel by the end of the day.

By now it was past time for Mother to explain the rest of the girlie things to me. She finally handed me a book. She obviously didn't want to tell me anything I might get interested in. Of course that made me all the more curious. The dictionary was no help either, so I put it down and went sneaking around in *Gray's Anatomy.* All it had in it were big words and cross-sections.

Then we moved to Columbia, Missouri, too late for me to be tested and put into the proper math level. I ended up with the slower kids because there was more room in the inn. I soon learned my teacher was the master trickster when it came to making students learn and was also kind enough to keep his eyes off growing-up irregularities.

I signed up for the band, which took me out of the building and into a side street, where we girls had to learn how to march in tight skirts. It was equally hard to keep our mouthpieces out of our noses and our eyes on jiggling music. Dodging fallen tree limbs, I thought of Mother and the horse piles. Where we were going to perform later was a mystery to me.

It turned out we were to play for some late-season high school football games, dressed in scratchy uniforms in the freezing cold, with icicles hanging from our noses. Unfortunately, bladders filled up rather quickly under those conditions. Once, in an effort to locate a bathroom, I accidentally found myself in the boys' dressing room. I acted like I was the Queen of England looking for someone and meandered back out the door, red-faced and looking straight ahead.

Even though I could look a grass snake in the eye, it was almost impossible for me to fearlessly stand up and perform in front of an indoor audience, showing my skinny legs and trying to keep my clarinet reed from squeaking. Worse yet, I chose "Flight of the Bumblebee" as my first solo. At one-fourth speed, the bumblebee sounded as if it had been shot with mace. Prompting from my band teacher to imagine everyone in the audience wearing long, red underwear only made me snicker when I saw the principal.

By then I had warmed up my vocal chords singing in junior choirs at church and was ready for Mrs. Schlotzhauer's chorus class. First I had to learn how to spell and to pronounce her name, the latter not an easy task, because you had to spit to get started. Between band and schpitting, I was having a wonderful time. It was this time in my life that I don't know what I would have done without my best friend, Barbara. She could play the piano like no one else in school, no matter what grade they were in. When any of us needed someone to accompany us, she was there. With her playing for me, I started getting braver about performing in front of an audience. Pretty soon we started getting braver in general.

We only lived a block apart. When we'd get home, we'd get on the phone and start conjuring up crazy stuff about our classmates, until our parents started laughing at us. Somehow our school newspaper got wind of us, and the sponsor asked us if we'd like to write the column for our class, which we ended up doing clear into high school. Our classmates should have started trembling when it was announced that I was to become co-editor my senior year.

I'm glad I didn't have gym class with Barb, because she was strong and well-built, and I was a ninety-eight pound weakling forced to play dodge ball against girls sired by gorillas. All I knew about dodge ball and softball was that I needed to duck when I saw a ball coming. The only reason I passed the class was because I made A's on my tests and took showers.

English and social studies was a big class, and I found myself on the back row next to a really cute boy, but was a bit disappointed when he told me he had loved someone else since the third grade. That particular year, he had occasionally raced home to a place in the bushes near her house, just to be able to see her walk in her back door.

It was no secret I loved birds. Since I had a pet grackle (blackbird) that I had rescued as a baby, the boy told me about his brother's pet crow who hated the woman next door. The crow would wait for days for it to rain on her clothes hanging outside on the line. After a mud puddle would form directly underneath, he'd fly over and pull all the clothespins off, hysterically screeching as each garment fell into the mud. I told the boy that when I let my grackle out of his cage, he'd run the dog off, take a bath in her water, and eat her food. When people came over, he'd land on top of their heads and rummage around as if he were searching for lice. He'd slip around on bald people's heads looking like some drunk on skis.

The fellow and I liked our teacher, but found ourselves distracted when she wrote on the board, as she moved her mouth around like a horse eating corn. Teenage rumor had it that she chewed coffee grounds. Our civics teacher was another oddity to us, as she was near retirement and had never been married. A boy mistakenly called her Mrs. Allen, and she snapped at him saying, "I'm *Miss* Allen, I've never had a man, and I don't intend to get one!"

Some years later, she married a widower in his late eighties. He sat on the front porch of their house and rocked while she worked in the garden, her wobbling rear end greeting Worley Street traffic. She died a year later. Probably couldn't stand all the excitement.

Home economics was the most fun. Mother had just taught me how to sew, stating that if I wanted any new clothes, I would have to make them myself. Our teacher had no inhibitions about tattling on herself, and during a segment on personal grooming, confessed she always dried her hair in the oven. Our first cooking project was making a volcano out of mashed potatoes, with gravy oozing from the center. The local newspaper even came and took a picture of us and wrote up an article for an upcoming issue. I knew they had to be hurting for news.

My last rite of passage from puberty was completed the night I got my first kiss from Paul behind the barn at the county fair. He was gentle, sweet, and as pure of thought and action as any 50's girl would want. He could also play the trumpet in our band without puffing out his cheeks or making barnyard noises.

Before going into ninth grade, I had achieved first chair in the band, with only three years of clarinet under my belt. Janet, who was much more diligent at practicing than I was, had a year of trumpet and was already fairly proficient on the flute by age eleven. Therefore, Mother was always on the lookout for musical opportunities for us, with or without our knowledge. She saw an ad from Stephens College, which she stuffed under my nose. They were looking for a clarinet player for their orchestra.

"I'm too young for them!" I said.

"Why don't you try it and see. They might be desperate, and besides, they'll give free music lessons in exchange for playing with them."

Surprisingly, I got the position, even after telling them I was only fourteen and inexperienced and had been kissed only once by a boy. I played clarinet for a very short time, because the first semester opera score needed a bass clarinet player. They handed me their horn, and one rehearsal later, I was honking like a Canada goose. Then the big news came. They needed a second oboe player for *Amahl and the Night Visitors*, and would I mind learning the oboe for the performance in December of the next year. They had a spare in a closet. I was already suspicious of their oboe because it was made by a trumpet company. A metal band circled a crack in the wood on the bottom half. Crack or no crack, I accepted it and rushed off to public school music camp to learn how to play it.

Mr. Murphy, the orchestra conductor and also St. Louis Symphony first chair French horn player, had been generous in his praise of my clarinet and bass clarinet playing, even though he had to order me special music since I couldn't read the bass clef. By November, he eased off calling me a musical assassin during *Amahl* rehearsals, even though I knew my oboe playing made the hair in his ears curl. I wasn't too thrilled about being called a musical assassin, but so far the opportunities were outweighing the negatives.

When *Amahl* was over, he asked me to stay on as second oboist, questioning me if I knew anyone who could play the piccolo. "If you have a piccolo, I have an eleven-year-old sister who could," I said. She got the position. One performance night, I watched her with only lights from our music stands showing our faces. Beside her was her faculty music teacher. On the other side were two Stephens students, and behind her was the St. Louis Symphony bassoonist, brought in with some of his peers to fill in for missing parts. What an experience for a girl in sixth grade who climbed trees with boys for recreation.

Playing second oboe at Stephens left me some time to watch the action on stage during opera rehearsals. After awhile, Father and I agreed there was almost a pattern to operas. Some dastardly, dagger-carrying villain with dark hair, singing bass, usually got himself into some kind of trouble during the first act. Consequently he either had to hide behind the drapes or in the bushes to spy, or because others were looking for him. The alto usually played a second fiddle role as the maid, someone's mother, or a nun. The tenor and the soprano were the hero and heroine and had to make sure the bushes they were hiding behind weren't the same as those of the villain.

In the end, someone either stabbed or shot himself or someone else did it for him. Or if that were too common, he jumped off a balcony, taking his lover with him. If that didn't work, some dread disease or poison did, causing him to lie down while he panted through his last songs, with or without wailing choral accompaniment and chain rattling.

At school the music department had no place for such sultry plots, but wasn't without its excitement. Our band director confessed that the year before, he got so involved with some wild hair piece, he got carried away with his own directing and ran the baton up his nose.

Janet and I thought Mr. Murphy was getting delightfully unpredictable. One afternoon he came in five minutes late, hurriedly explaining that the motor had fallen out of his car in the middle of Highway 40. When our ten minute break came, he jokingly yelled, "To the gaming tables, to the opium," as we raced toward the restrooms.

Once he had to take the train to Columbia via Centralia. He showed up red-faced, sputtering that they had to stop the train because there were two diamond thieves on it and no Centralia police available to catch them. "The Centralia police were all too busy out there putting nickels in parking meters!" he roared.

The highlight was the day he came in with his pants held on with a clothesline rope with a bow tied in the front. We stifled laughter for thirty minutes before he caught us. Putting his baton down, he said, "You're laughing because my pants are tied on with a rope. I lost my belt," and went on conducting.

There was still more to come; however, I eventually left the orchestra in the middle of my freshman year in college. The next time I saw him was when I was thirty years old and dean of girls at Parkwood High School in Joplin. The St. Louis Symphony had come to Parkwood to put on a concert. He had retired from playing with them and had taken over the job of on-tour manager. We sat amid a pile of instrument cases, laughing and reminiscing, while the Symphony played. It was such a wonderful feeling to be relating as an adult to my funny, talented, and unpredictable mentor who had helped me get so far into the music world.

I was about to enter high school. Sophomores had to wear little green and white beanies for a few weeks, just long enough to develop semi-permanent scalp itch. No one would tell me what would happen if I didn't wear mine, but I suspected it would be something to avoid, when I saw some upper classmen making a beanie-less sophomore boy kneel down and propose to a downtown parking meter.

My favorite class was Spanish. Our teacher was not only a model instructor, but a model dresser. We almost couldn't believe her the morning she confessed to laying the day's clothes out in the closet the night before so she wouldn't have to worry about dressing in the dark, only to discover she'd put her straight skirt on wrong-side out as well as upside-down.

After a year in high school, I decided I wasn't going to march in any tight skirt anymore with an oboe reed up one nostril. I signed up for orchestra as the only oboe player, giving me a chance to do solo parts. By then I had worn off some of my stage fright playing in a band and orchestra at summer music camp.

I had gotten so tired of practicing my music lessons that I had been turning my music upside down, making it sound like a spook show with black-haired women running through the moss. When I was sixteen, Mr. Murphy figured I needed some revitalization and got me a scholarship to send me to Chautauqua, New York, for a summer of youth orchestra playing and music lessons. The man who sat next to me on the train was a spy for the CIA or something and couldn't even tell his wife about what he did. We talked for half the night before we finally dozed off in our seats. When I got off the train, I ran up to Mr. Murphy, and without thinking said, "Let me tell you about the man I slept with last night!"

Oboe lessons had been arranged for me with the English horn player from the Metropolitan Opera Company Symphony Orchestra.

If that weren't exciting enough, he had a fetish for spiders. When we finished, we trudged a short way into the woods looking for them. Equally exciting was trying out for and getting a soprano position with the Chautauqua Symphonic Choir, composed of adults from all over the United States. We went from *Oklahoma* to doing Beethoven in German, taking me back to schpitting again.

I was standing in line in the Chautauqua Post Office one morning, when I recognized nineteen-year-old Van Cliburn standing in front of me. He had just put on a concert and was being touted by the long-hairs as an upcoming great. I noticed his fingers, which seemed twelve inches long next to my stubby ones. No wonder he could play.

I was rooming at the Disciples of Christ headquarters with two Stephens College girls. After our rehearsals were over, we would go eat at a local hotel harboring mostly older people, where we could get in a hot food line for a pretty tasty and affordable meal. Since the hotel residents must have all gone to finishing school like I eventually did, I changed into a skirt before going to supper. My roommates didn't, and I tried to convince them that going to dinner in their shorts in a nice hotel full of properly dressed adults might not be appropriate. Somehow they weren't impressed with that.

One evening the head waiter came up and asked me if I would step out of the food line. He led me aside where I could see all of the other waiters smiling and peeking out of a door.

He said, "We all want to tell you something. Compared to your two friends, you have made a big impression on us and on our hotel guests by taking the time to honor us by dressing up for us every evening. We just want to thank you and tell you how much we appreciate it!" Six young men smiled and waved at me from the doorway. I smiled back and tried hard to hold back grateful tears.

I never forgot that moment. It added credence to the day in seventh grade, when after years of my mother making me wear slacks like a boy so I wouldn't catch cold, even in the slightest of chilly weather, I decided that every day I would try to be feminine and dress like a lady. Mother's intentions had been good, but she never realized how hurt I felt psychologically by it during most of grade school. After that, I also swore that never again would I let something like that control my emotions, including my father's quick temper, which for no reason, I had started to copy. *I decided to choose to be a happy person* and both decisions put me on a path to life that I never left.

The next time I went to a music camp, I had to take the bus and wait two hours in Kansas City. An old drunk on the other side kept lighting up the filter ends of his cigarettes, stinking up the whole bus station. I was allergic to cigarette smoke, but the scenario was too funny for me to want to move.

Music and art camp in Lawrence, Kansas, came with a terrible heat wave and no air conditioning. To keep from drowning in his own perspiration, the band director wore a white towel around his neck every day, only to be surprised one afternoon by the fifty boys in the band grinning and sporting white towels around theirs.

I was fascinated by a Mexican art student named Lupita. Since I was already into learning Spanish, we connected like glue. She spent quite a bit of time staring at a picture of her boyfriend, Carlos, that she had in the window. One afternoon I found Carlos' picture facing the rain outdoors. "I mad at heem!" she said.

Right before the 10 p.m. dorm curfew, it wasn't unusual to see an abundance of necking and kissing going on in the bushes, but it was a bit odd to see Lupita alone behind one of them. Before I could say anything, she said, "Shut up! I taking lessons!"

We gave her a birthday party before we all left, giving her some nylon hose and a frilly crinoline petticoat. The hose embarrassed her and she hid them under the covers, but she fell in love with the petticoat, put it on over her slacks, showed it to everyone in the dorm, and disappeared outside with it still on.

My roommates told me later they wished they had gotten a picture of that. Instead they conned me into letting them take a picture of me with my first and only unlit cigarette in my mouth. I balked at first, but after promising me they would never show it to my parents, I reveled in my one glorious moment of looking like a wanton woman.

This was my last summer music camp. I was beginning to wonder if I was destined to be a musician for the rest of my life, especially after I was told by the orchestra leader that I might qualify for a music scholarship to KU after another year. However, camps after that were all church ones held at Christian College in St. Clair Hall, one of their oldest buildings. One summer a bat took up residence on first floor, causing a voluntary building evacuation of screaming girls as he raced from one end of the hall to the other.

Obviously too big for a mayonnaise jar, I had to find something else, so I picked up a huge head scarf and caught him on the third try as he flew by. I wasn't prepared for warring sharp claws and teeth, and it was quite a feat to keep him from biting me before I could dump him in a shoe box and turn him loose outside. One of the girls came back and asked if she could sleep all night with me, figuring if we were going to be attacked by aliens again, she might at least have someone to protect her.

By the time I was a junior, we were hearing that integration would be enforced and new students from Douglas School would soon be coming to Hickman. For me, that was going to be a thrilling challenge, as my parents had always been proponents of equality. I looked forward to that day and hoped my classmates did too, but with some feeling of apprehension in case someone didn't. A couple of black girls appeared in some of my classes, and there was a period of studied looks, smiles, and a lot of silence as we sized each other up and waited to see what would happen. Nothing did, and school for the most part went on as usual.

I hurried to make friends, and it wasn't long before I found myself invited into some of their activities. One of the girls had an older sister who was expecting a baby soon, and I was asked to come to her baby shower. One of her other sisters quizzed her in the middle of it, asking, "Hey woman, how come you got pregnant? I thought you kicked him out of the house!"

"I did, but he got back in through the basement window."

Next came participation in one of the local black churches during Sunday morning services. I sat in awe of a totally different kind of music from the classical style I was so used to. I sang with them; however, I couldn't quite get into the mood of all the swinging, swaying, halleluias, and amens.

One of the black girls and I got along exceedingly well. She was a senior and due to get married soon, and before long, asked me if I would be one of her bridesmaids. That thrilled me to death, but something told me I'd better check out things at home. When I confronted Mother with it, I got a very disappointing response. She made some feeble excuses about what people might think and that it might cast a shadow over their position in society. I talked this over with my friend who was gracious about it. I still wanted to do something for her, so I asked if I could make her wedding dress. In addition to the fun of doing it, I knew it would place her in and out of our house while I was fitting her.

That worked well. Mother also welcomed her and made no comments about her being seen in the neighborhood or going in and out of our house. On the girl's wedding day, not only did a huge number of white students show up, but the president of the student body. After I told Mother, it seemed to break the ice for her. From then on, I saw a multitude of nationalities and colors enter my parents' home, many becoming almost part of the family.

Toward my senior year, I was anxious to be earning a little extra money on my own, since my parents couldn't afford another music camp for me. My new boyfriend, Vince, found me a job at the Lenoir retirement home for full-time Christian service workers, housed in one long building called the Manor. He thought I might like to work there because his mother had a job there as a nurse. I was given a room vacated by an older lady who was slowly dying in the convalescent end of the floor, and was to work in the laundry and wait tables during all three meals.

Vince and his twin sister, Kay, were new arrivals in town, and we had connected because we were all into music at church. They had come late in their parents' lives, which must have been a merry chase for two older parents with other children mostly grown and gone. The two confessed that twins could do what one child couldn't. If one child couldn't reach a light switch to click it off and on, two could by dragging a coffee table under it and climbing up onto it. Two could also outfox a baby-sitter by running off in opposite directions.

However, that didn't diminish Vince's urges later to torment his sister. One day when she was practicing on her piano, he sneaked up behind her with some chicken feet he'd conned from their father who had brought the bird home to be strangled, de-feathered, and eaten for supper. Vince placed the claws on Kay's shoulder and pulled on the tendons to help them grasp. Her screams were right in tune with the song she had been practicing. Their mother had learned to take this and a lot of other things in stride, especially in later years, when they affectionately started calling her Old Swivel Hips.

So I packed up my coolest clothes and joined Old Swivel Hips, where every business day was laundry day. We did it all, except for a very hot summer day, when we found that a resident had beaten us to it. A basement clothesline contained seven near-winter garments of hers, just beginning to dry.

"Honey, you did this all yourself? We would have gladly done your washing for you," I said.

"Sweetie, that's just what I had on this morning. I felt a bug in my britches and I had to get him out."

One very old gentleman was another issue. We had to soak his handkerchiefs in straight bleach for twenty minutes before we dared to put them in the washing machine. He had year- round nasal drip, which seemed to grip him at mealtimes. When he was through blowing and the meal was over, he would sit at the table and take that same handkerchief, remove his false teeth, and carefully clean them with it, making sure he ran the handkerchief's edges between some of the teeth.

That didn't faze a quiet, ninety-year-old lady who sat nearby, as her eyesight was failing, but not to the extent that she couldn't see up close to do some fine oil paintings for the dining room. I complimented her on a beautiful painting of a cabbage she had done.

"On the contrary, my dear, it was a fine cabbage."

A missionary lady, who had spent a lifetime doing without, understandably began trying to con me into smuggling in her favorite butter-brickle ice cream or slices of cold tongue. I had never seen anyone cook tongue before, and I kept thinking about our dog, knowing where his tongue had been.

I loved working with these older folks. They told funny and exciting stories; yet I had to watch out for a few of them not to get trapped by their mile-long dialogs and aging brain misfires. One old fellow, who truly loved his ailing and withered-looking wife, kept stalking me in the basement hallways as if he were a sixteen year old in hot pursuit of a new girlfriend. I finally convinced him we should meet by the parlor piano, where I could sing for him and his wife when she was feeling up to it.

After I worked there for awhile, the dying lady graciously gave me permission to come through her room during my hour and a half break so I could go out onto the adjoining half-hidden patio and sun myself while I read a book. As she grew more delirious, she began to imagine that I had nothing on under my monster beach towel and was certain that some boy was climbing up the drain pipe every day for some illicit rendezvous.

So instead of going outdoors, I sat with her so she would have someone there to listen to her last visions of seeing her mother waiting for her somewhere out there. When Vince's mother would come with more medicine, she would graciously ask her to please stop, because she was ready to go. By the time I ended my summer's work, she was gone.

Back home again, Father told me that his uncle Roscoe had found out I could play the clarinet. He asked Father if I would be willing to look over an antique Albert system clarinet he had, to see if it could be repaired. He wanted to pass it down to his grandchildren as soon as they grew up and quit acting like house apes. Fascinated, I repaired it myself and got it playing again, even though it was so old it sounded like it was coming from the bottom of a beer barrel. I gloated over it and kept it hidden for several years until Roscoe gave us the word it was safe to give back. Mother ranted for weeks when she found out the now responsible grandson who inherited it had made a lamp out of it. However, she more than forgave him some years later and invited him to come live with them while he went to medical school.

Roscoe had a brother, Jim, who lived in the old family homestead and didn't know a musical note from a good moose call. We had heard he was quite an eccentric; in fact, Mother claimed it didn't even have an outhouse and that he did his business behind a mulberry bush. Mother was sometimes prone to exaggeration, but the first time we visited him, my antennae went up anyway. We weren't invited in, so Janet and I had to stay in the car, painfully aware that the mulberry bush was out of sight, so we had no way of estimating the height of the piles behind it. Decades later, when it became my job to try to sell the family property, I asked Father what had happened to the old house.

"The termites ate it, and it fell in," he said.

Mother had her own breed of relatives who were full of the devil and always laughing over something. The eastern Missouri ones didn't play any musical instruments, but they had their own ideas about entertainment. Her aunt Lucy and uncle Lloyd were the epitome of country hospitality, even if you came without warning. You did that at your own risk, as there was always a parakeet named Mortimer loose in the house.

Mortimer III loved to eat breakfast with guests, running across their fried eggs and heavily jellied toast, and then landing back in his seed-infested cage. He would return with seeds glued to his feet and swoop to the floor, where he would fiddle with a knife handle under the kitchen table for a couple of hours. Later he'd get the rest of the seeds off his feet by diving in and out of the fish bowl. He'd go to the bathroom to dry off and spend some part of the day looking at himself in the mirror.

Aunt Lucy had a room that she called the Chamber of Horrors. She claimed no one would risk going in there with her. She didn't dare take anything out of it, or the whole rest of the room would fall into the hall. I'd heard of Fibber McGee's closet, but my visions of it didn't hold a candle to this one. Somehow she managed to do her ironing in there, with only half of the ironing board available; the rest consumed with boxes with things hanging out of them that looked like they didn't belong to the twentieth century. The more I thought about Aunt Lucy and all the bizarre things that went on at her house, the more I was convinced she, more than any of her other five siblings, was the clown among the older Patton brothers and sisters. No wonder she and Mother got along so well.

When we visited, Janet and I got to sleep upstairs, where we could practice on our instruments if we wanted to. That made the birds outdoors sing, especially an irresponsible mother robin, who would leave her husband on the nest to keep the eggs warm while she cavorted. Uncle Lloyd didn't think he ought to have to do that and told him about it one Sunday after church when he was looking out the back door.

The last I remember of that room was the day a big, black, hairy spider decided to come calling on us. Janet and I weren't prone to killing spiders, but this one had an attitude, so we dug him a grave in Aunt Lucy's powder box and buried him. We thought about playing taps on Janet's trumpet.

It was time to quit thinking about silly relatives, endless music rehearsals, and spider revenge, and direct attention toward graduating from high school. I was still clueless about what I was going to major in, even though most of my classmates, as well as my parents, figured it would be music. Although several of us would be going to the same junior college, I knew I would miss my buddies destined to scatter elsewhere. We said our farewells at Hickman's first-ever, well-chaperoned all-night party held in our First Christian Church basement. Someone must have thought the Lord would rid us of any sinful thoughts if they held it there, which was certainly a waste of time for the better part of us who were totally naïve. Those who weren't just had to tough it out.

Pet grackle

Chapter 4

CHRISTIAN COLLEGE AND THE CAVALCADE OF CHARACTERS

After I graduated from high school, I went on to Christian College just a few blocks away and at least picked up where I left off with my high school Spanish classes. At the end of my first year there, Janet brought her yearbook home from her sophomore year in high school. Eagerly I looked for familiar faces, only to encounter Elvira Sloop Gritch lurking in most of the important pictures. She had mop hair, a contorted face, queer glasses, and the wrong clothes. She even looked like she might stink.

Janet hadn't seen her around school. I got out my magnifying glass. No moles, no scars, no unusual teeth, no clues. Then I stumbled upon a telltale picture of a girl I knew. She had the same nose, earlobes, ankles, teeth, and elbows. I wondered if the yearbook sponsor had been in cahoots. Or asleep. I should have sent someone a congratulatory letter for pulling it off.

Janet kept asking me what college was like. Christian College in 1956 was any girl's dream. We town girls were given a small apartment, where we could hang out and study. Nevertheless, for the first six weeks, we felt it didn't make up for all the fellowship the dorm girls seemed to be having.

We were essentially in a scholarly Christian finishing school with set rules. No going to church up the street without a hat, hose, and heels, or the dean of women would surely be hiding in the bushes waiting to catch us. There were many thou shalt nots. Thou shalt not go down the fire escape at night and into the loving arms of a university boy waiting at the bottom. Special assemblies pointed to more. Thou shalt not stab thy food with a fork, as if attempting to spear a mouse, but instead, use it to scoop up and delicately put crawly lettuce, wobbly figs, and squirming peas into thy mouth. Thou shalt not wear earrings with jeans, nor saddle shoes with after-five dresses. Thou shalt not sneak into the chapel at night and hold séances. Thou shalt attend chapel every week and properly dressed.

It's a good thing there weren't any thou shalt nots about having fun with our teachers, or I would have had to quit on the spot and go to the university. I loved tormenting Dr. Long, who taught zoology and made funny comparisons, like the class skeleton probably belonging to some old baboon or maybe his ex-girlfriend's dead uncle.

I didn't know how much Dr. Long enjoyed my voice, until one evening I ran into him at the high school where his wife worked and where they had both heard me sing. With a genuinely serious look on his face, he told me he eventually wanted me to sing at his funeral. Proud and pleased, I blurted out, "Gladly!" He laughed so hard he couldn't stop, and for years, he heckled me about being overjoyed about crooning to his corpse.

Then a long time afterwards, when I was visiting Mother in the hospital, she said Dr. Long was recovering in a room upstairs. He had been shot by an itinerant man whom he had generously hired to work on his property so he could earn a few dollars to buy food. When I stepped into his room, his eyes focused for a moment, and he started laughing.

"It's not time yet! It's not time yet! Go home!"

I loved Sid Larson's art class above all others, because he was indescribably funny and could make artistic purses out of sows' ears. He didn't discover his art talent until some time into medical school and suddenly changed majors. I found my forte was not oil painting, as I made the power plant on back campus look like the Queen Mary; however, charcoaling I got down to a fine art. When he challenged us to draw anything we wanted around the buildings, I drew a big dent into his car's rear fender.

I had already been singing in the church choir since ninth grade and eventually kept on until I left home in 1960. It was directed by Tom Mills, who was director of the University Singers. Tom started calling me Andrew to keep me humble, which led into a long succession of self-appointed professors in charge of keeping me humble until I turned fifty-six years old.

Tom told us about his grouchy old neighbor lady, who had stomped over to his house one day, swearing his son had stuffed grass in her mailbox so she couldn't get her bills. Tom thought about that for awhile and suggested to her that if that would keep him from getting his bills, he'd have his son stuff some in his mailbox too.

One week Tom decided the choir had slipped a notch and made up a first grade attendance chart with gold stars to paste on for Wednesday nights and Sundays. At the bottom he wrote,

"He Who Has Fewest Stars Must Buy Choir Director Expensive Gift!" Sunday morning we started pasting stars on each other's foreheads and begging for extra credit.

Dr. Lemmon, the minister who had been there forever, thought this was pretty amusing. What wasn't so funny was that skirts were starting to go up, morals were continuing to go down, and some of the younger people were starting to come to church in their lawn clothes. He began one of his sermons, "We have just entered into the age of studied tackiness," which brought down the house.

One day as I was walking into the church, I saw that the woman ahead of me was wearing tattered hose patched with bits of white adhesive tape covering her thin, hairy legs. Later I learned that she and her very musically talented daughter, Callie, had spent some part of their lives sleeping on park benches somewhere else and scraping just enough money together to be able to afford an ancient car.

Callie played clarinet in the city band and was technically way ahead of me when we got to comparing our first three years. We became good friends, and soon she came to sing in the choir and to join our college youth group.

That went along for some time, until one Sunday, when I was directing the youth group's morning hymns, Callie came in late. She had dyed her hair with bright green food coloring with under-the-fingernails to match. I was having a hard time not snorting all over my music. My mind raced to our chancel choir performance less than one hour away and the stir this could cause in a college-dominated, sophisticated congregation. She walked right into the choir loft with the rest of us, while the congregation sucked air. I thought about putting a star on her forehead.

Callie wasn't the only town character. An elderly professor's wife had somehow lost it, either before or after her husband had died. She lived in a haunted-looking house with weeds growing up in the front yard and would wander about town with her glasses on top of her head and her tennis shoes tied to her feet with string.

Father was of Puritan stock and wouldn't stop the car to pick up another woman even if she were drowning in the rain. So one evening at supper, Mother warned Father about the lady, as she had started standing on a certain intersection and getting into people's cars when they stopped. There was a long silence, and Father started turning several colors of red. Smelling a rat, Mother asked, "Do you know something about that?"

"She got in my car," he mumbled. Then it came out. He had stopped at that stop sign, and suddenly she was in the back seat of his car. He roared, "What do you think you're doing!"

"I'm getting in your car."

"And just where do you think you're going?"

"I'm going wherever you're going, honey."

"Get out!" But she wouldn't. "I'm going to the police station!" he bellowed. He did, and that's where he made her get out.

Mother had experienced her own encounters with the lady at AAUW meetings. The lady would come to finger-food luncheons and bring her doggie bag. Once she went up to Mother, lowered her glasses, and puffed up like an adder, asking, "Have you paid your dues?"

My second year in college, my seven-year-old grackle suddenly died from some type of neurological disorder. I was too broken-hearted to even bury him, so Mother suggested I wrap him in waxed paper and put him in the refrigerator until I was ready. He lay in state there for a week, nestled against some cheese that was turning into living Technicolor.

I looked backwards, remembering when he was almost grown and we took him and his sister on vacation with us to California. Mother warned me we might not get them past the California border inspection. What did she think they were going to classify them as, anyway? Fruit? Vegetables? They had eaten all their lice. I covered up their cage with a big map, but that didn't fool the inspector. He uncovered them, his face screwed up like that of an orangutan inspecting the bottom side of a tarantula. He gave me a dirty look and waved us on even farther into the Sierras, where the male got car sick and threw up in my shoe.

I remembered all the times I had let the birds out to play on that trip, each time coming back to their cage when called. Even when a flock of redwing blackbirds came down to play with them, they stayed with us after their wild friends flew off. I cried when I thought of the day we were visiting in Reno, when they were playing in a friend's yard, and the male jumped up on the porch railing, acting like he was squawking for a grape. In reality he was trying to warn me his sister was being eaten by a cat.

The day he stayed gone all day in Salt Lake City, he lost his freedom. After that we let him out to play in the house, where he invented his own fun. He would get right up to my face and open his beak up wide, hoping I would open my mouth so he could see my bubble gum. A couple of times he snatched it up and flew off. One time I gave him a grapefruit rind, with the round side up, to see what he would do with it. He got up on top of it and danced around a few times and then started punching it full of holes. Each time he would clean his feathers with the stuff he got on his beak, until he looked like the epitome of a bad hair day. It took several baths in the dog dish to get cleaned up again.

Toward the last, when the dog had experienced a couple of days of jumping out of her bed yelping, I finally got down to see if there was a sticker in her bed. I happened to look through a knothole on the boarded-up side of the bird's cage next to the dog bed, only to see a beady yellow eye looking back at me, next to a sharp beak full of white dog hairs. It marked the end of my longest era with wild birds, but I knew if I ever had another chance to rescue a baby, I would do it.

It was time to decide on my major. In almost two years, I had made no progress. I pored over my transcript. The most hours on it were in Spanish. Not knowing what else to do, I sighed and prepared to head for MU to major in that.

That wasn't all I needed to learn. Soon after I started school at Christian, I began dating a nice young MU student from St. Louis named Jack Hamilton, who ran around with some of my male friends in our college age church group. He was about my height, so that our noses could touch without stretching. My nose was too big, and his was beautiful and turned up. His hair was almost red, and I kept looking at him about five o'clock shadow time, to see if his whiskers were any redder. There was hope - just checking out genes before I got too serious. I wanted someone taller, but most of the taller ones were goofballs. Underneath, I was even beginning to feel sad and a little afraid that the right man would never come along before I got too old.

Jack was one of the few who had a car, and during the time I was dating another fellow, he would offer to take us both home after our evening church activities. I found out later, he was doing it just to be able to be around me. After six months, he proposed. He saw me hesitate and his eyes filled with tears. In a weak moment, I told myself I couldn't disappoint this nice fellow and I said yes. I wanted to say no, but there was no one else. I swore to myself that I could learn to love him.

If Jack ever had any unholy intentions, he had to stifle them, as I was still as dumb as a rock and not much past dictionary definitions and *Gray's Anatomy.* Finally he asked me very kindly, "Before we get married, would you please go read a book?"

I found a sociology book in the library, but all the juicy pages had been torn out. I went through science labs, hunting for pictures. Then I found the book that picked up where Webster's Dictionary had left off. I was horrified. Not in a million years was a man going to do that to me.

In disbelief, I got a pair of scissors, some tape, a ruler, and a piece of typing paper and made a scale model. I hid it under the bed where my parents were afraid to look anyway. I got it out from time to time and pored over measurements. I even showed it to Janet. She was only sixteen and might as well have advance warning. I shouldn't have worried. I found out later that all some of my male age-mates knew about girls was what they saw on the leaflets inside their sisters' tampon boxes.

Years later, when I was teaching psychology in high school and dealing with the chapter on dating and marriage, I discreetly told my students how pitifully dumb I had been clear up to age nineteen. They came back the next day and told me how I had ruined their chemistry class the next hour. "Who, me?" I asked. "How did you figure that?"

"Well, the first thing our teacher did was to draw a big huge test tube on the blackboard and leave it there, and he couldn't figure out why we were laughing at him all hour."

When I was a junior in college, suddenly one night, my sweet and funny sister, Janet, stepped out of the high school orchestra pit and into the audience to take an intermission break to visit with Jack and me who had come to hear her play. Her demeanor had changed into one of concern and suspicion that her flute teacher was after her. Other strange comments made us wonder what was going on. The next day, more odd behavior was noticed, and Mother started quizzing me about it. The bottom line was a diagnosis of schizophrenia by a woman psychiatrist who began treating her so she could at least barely finish high school on time.

Janet had already experienced more than she bargained for with a serious back surgery when she was nine years old, to correct some curvature in her spine. I never saw a little girl take something like that so gracefully. Her great attitude and ability to resist complaining eventually carried her through into adulthood, where she continued to successfully go on with her life in spite of a new world of medications needed to keep her going. Without missing a beat, she went on to graduate from Stephens College as one of their first graduates to receive a bachelor of fine arts. From there, she went on to Eastman for a master's in music, and later to MU for another master's in library science.

Mother really ran scared about what might happen to Janet during those college years. She was afraid that if Janet didn't get what she wanted, it would throw her further into an abyss of mental illness that she might not be able to crawl out of. Consequently I saw her get special privileges that I had not gotten, such as getting her hair done at the beauty shop, while I had to do my own. She was sent to one of the two finest music schools in the nation, while I had to stay at home to go to college. She went to Switzerland for some special experiences, whereas I never had the chance to leave the country.

Someone asked me one day why I wasn't resentful of all the favoritism. Why should I be? This was their problem, not mine to work through. I had my own life ahead of me and could only wish them well on their tortuous journey.

Then a long period began of seldom seeing Janet, either because of our busy lives at our college and public school jobs, or because we were too many miles apart. I always regretted the lost years that we might have had together. I missed her tendency to come up with funny one-liners like Father did and her ability to see the humorous side when nobody else could. But then it was probably just as well, as her bent toward mischief was more creative than mine, and we might have both ended up in jail.

Chapter 5

HORSEPLAY ON THE ROAD TO ACADEMIA

I was almost twenty and thinking about death. It all started when the governor put Father in charge of the disposition of dead bodies for the State of Missouri. Cadavers suddenly got interesting again. I started considering my own death and even donating my body to medical science, or at least becoming an organ donor.

But what if I lived to be 98 like Father's half-sister eventually did? Who would want a kidney about ready to celebrate a centennial? People needed things that were currently working. Maybe I should just be satisfied with lying in the university's cadaver room, where my children and what's left of my classmates could come and visit. A couple of my classmates were students of Father's anyway, and it could remind them of old times.

Grandpa Lowrance died while I was at MU. He was too old to be an organ donor, so Father "had him pickled," and went to Salt Lake City to tend to the funeral, empty the house, bring home Grandpa's love letters and other loot, and figure out what to do with Grandma and Polly. Grandma still didn't like Polly, but she didn't want to turn loose of him because Grandpa had loved him so much.

Having Polly at our house was a great reunion for Mother, who now had him back after twenty-four years. Having Grandma was another issue. Until an addition could be added to the house for her, I gave her my room and moved to the basement.

She would come to breakfast, and halfway through grace, she would yell, "Where are my teeth?" and have to go back and get them. Once she picked up a copy of Mother's *Reader's Digest* in Spanish, and unknown to Mother, spent an hour trying to read it.

"Is this how the *Reader's Digest* is now?" she asked her.

"Yep."

"Then I'd better cancel my subscriptions to my friends."

Grandma had always wanted to come stay with us long enough to hear Dr. Lemmon preach and was overjoyed knowing she would finally get to do it. Her first Sunday, she dressed up and found her a permanent spot in a pew. Halfway through the sermon, her eyes closed, her lower jaw dropped down, and her upper teeth came loose and crashed down to meet her lower ones. There she sat, Sunday after Sunday, with two rows of teeth on the bottom, snoring, weaving, and bobbing, and looking like some distorted Cheshire cat. Soon there was a vacant spot six people wide in any direction.

Mother left Grandma to her own devices for quite a while, but eventually made good progress toward leading her into "sinful ways." She managed to get her to the beauty shop, where they cut off two feet of her white hair that had been tied up in a bun. Then Mother conned her into getting a permanent. On my wedding day, Aunt Lucy, who could charm a witch, got ahold of her and said, "Grandma, you can't be seen up front at Ann's wedding without any lipstick."

"Okay!"

I was none the wiser about Lucy's attack on Grandma. When I walked down the aisle, there she was, proudly smiling, with bright red lipstick running up into both nostrils.

These were years when many of our friends were getting married too. To show our undying affection for them, Jack and I organized a posse to decorate their getaway cars and apartments. We got so good at it, we were even enlisted by people we didn't know. The rules were to do nothing destructive and nothing that couldn't be satisfactorily cleaned up in five minutes.

The first victims were a challenge, as they were to be living on the second floor of a tightly locked building. The police knew us and were watching and laughing from nearby bushes. We drove an old pickup truck up to the side of the building, hoisted a ladder, and went in the window. We found some clothesline, strung it across the room between two windows, and hung their underwear on it, leaving the blinds up and the lights on.

We got more creative while two of our best friends, Ginny and Steve, were on their honeymoon. They were to be staying with his folks after they returned. At the appointed hour, Steve's mother let us in, with cookies and Cokes waiting for us. We emptied the newlyweds' piggy bank and stuffed it full of sunflower seeds. We made a toilet seat out of a long, snaky balloon with the ends tied together, and a flush box cut out of poster paper. We attached them to a nearby oval wastebasket and placed it next to their bed along with a sign that said "For Emergency Use Only." We set the traditional alarm clock for some ungodly hour, pulled up the furnace grating, and nestled the clock on a horizontal piece of piping way down inside. I think it took them months to find all the rice we put in the toes of their socks. When they found out Steve's parents had let us in and fed us, they turned on them and did a number on their bathroom.

Later we got lured into some mischief involving a couple we didn't know. A friend had loaned them their garage to hide the getaway car in, and we could spy on the car from behind a curtain in the adjoining living room. During the ceremony, we tied a couple of old bedpans to the bumper and made garish eyelashes for the headlights. The car was locked, but Jack's father knew where a little pipe was that ran from under the hood into the car. He got a sickening sweet can of lilac room spray, pressed the button, and soon it fogged up the whole inside. When the couple returned and unlocked the car, they were bowled over by the smell. They figured someone had gotten inside their vehicle and they completely emptied their suitcases, hunting for trouble.

Some years later, when Jack's sister, Ruth, got married, she and Lee begged us to stay out of their car in exchange for giving us a key to the house. What an unexpected thrill! We set their table with the good silverware and two dog dishes. We hid fireplace wood in the piano bench, which they found about two years later. Their fly swatter went into the freezer. We stuffed Lee's one-piece army fatigues with crumpled newspapers, made a face out of a sack, put on a hat, and tied on boots, with one of them barely perched inside the toilet. We hung it on the shower rod, and when their little dog saw it, he stood up on his hind legs and pawed the air like he was giving homage to someone. After finding a needle and some white thread, I sewed up all of the fly fronts in Lee's underwear. Then we strategically laid out a his and a her set of underwear on the bedspread and stuffed the welcome mat under the covers. We were sorry later we didn't take pictures.

Somewhere amid all the horseplay, I found plenty of time to study. The Spanish department was outstanding, and I was surprised to find myself in some classes with both master's and doctoral candidates, who, by pulling some kind of an academic rope, could get graduate credit.

My most fun was with native Spanish professors, especially one whose accent was just as pronounced as it was the day she landed on U.S. shores from Cuba in a boat. It was hard to believe that a person with a Ph.D. would have to flee to the U.S. in such a way so as not to be murdered under the dictatorship of Fulgencio Batista. She told stories of how people were killed by being thrown into shark-infested waters running under a giant tower, and how a taxi ride might mean having to dodge bullets coming through the windows.

After she landed and had taught for awhile, she married one of her students, an older G.I. coming back to school after the war. They bought a little bite-sized dog named Perron, which in Spanish means great big dog. Perron liked to hide in the basement, where he would watch for legs to pass by the window up by the basement ceiling. If the legs were bare, he would stay quiet, but if they had men's pants on, he would bark and growl like he'd encountered a dragon.

Another professor prided himself on the Spanish poetry he wrote, until one day he recited something about an elephant in a violin case. A blind girl in the class gave him a thoughtful stare and announced, "You're on the decline!"

A third bachelor professor knew very little English. We ended up learning a lot more Spanish than we had anticipated, trying to find words to help him understand what to do or say, and what not to, when he was invited to a sorority party or when asked to go out by someone whose character he was unsure of.

I had fun in some of my other classes too. The philosophy professor tormented us with all kinds of perception versus reality games. He would hold up a pen and ask us if we thought it was a real pen, or if it was a pen just because we perceived it as a pen. I used that example years later, with a piece of chalk, when I was trying to teach scared older college students about where their perceptions of themselves were coming from. I would hold up the chalk and have them tell me what it was. Then I would take off my glasses and tell them how wrong they were, that it was indeed a cigarette. Then I would take out a match and try to light it, while they sat speechless.

"See how useless this piece of chalk is if I don't acknowledge what it really is and only try to use it as it's perceived? If you're trying to live your lives as others perceive you and not as the wonderful people you really are, see how useless you can begin to feel about yourselves?" Some author later wrote that he would like to turn a lion into a room full of philosophers and see just how long they would argue about whether it was a lion or just a perception of one.

In Life and Literature of the Old Testament, the professor was a Jewish gentleman who read from his Bible backwards. He was from the old country and knew thirty-six different languages and apologized profusely to me for not knowing Spanish.

Jack was studying landscape design, and in an attempt to possibly help him later, I took a class in landscape gardening. We went on field trips to identify plants, and on a trip to St. Louis, we were watching the ground for things we hadn't seen before. One of my classmates was smoking a catalpa pod and looking at the ground with a magnifying glass.

"Aha!" he said. "Sewerus pipus!"

Later in class, the professor apologized to us about the damp condition of our report cards. "My-two-year old daughter got ahold of them and dropped them in the toilet."

I learned that you were supposed to trim bushes around the house so they would grow out naturally and not look like Disneyland in the 1940s. In fact, I eventually had so much fun in that class, that I enrolled in Ornamental Trees. I was amazed that gingko trees came in male and female, and amused when a lady in the class pinched what she thought were little pine cones on an evergreen, and they squirmed.

In Nutrition and Health, I groaned with the rest of the class of summer school students, when the teacher came in dressed in the same dress for five days in a row. Other than that visual, I never forgot that vitamin C can be destroyed by heat or by oxygen, and that a stupid vitamin salesman, who popped a vitamin pill in his mouth with every customer visit to show how harmless vitamins were, was actually damaging his liver.

In Hygiene, I drew one page after another of colored guts, just like the ones my father had done on the blackboard with colored chalk in his biology lab. I loved the biological sciences, but when it came to chemistry, I was a washout. I didn't give a hoot about mixing chemicals to see if they would turn green, smell putrid, smoke, burst into flames, or eat chunks of round steak or live worms. The only thing I remembered from chemistry class was that the teacher's husband bragged about her light fluffy cakes (making me wonder, of course, about exactly what she put in them!). He hated light fluffy cakes and always wanted to get on top of one and stomp it down.

Right before I graduated from the University of Missouri with my Spanish degree, I still didn't have a clue as to what I would do with it.

I had sworn never to become a teacher, so I asked Johnny, who was sitting next to me in Spanish class. Johnny and I had been in the band together in high school, and we'd already been given the eyeball for having too much fun in class.

"You could be a translator in an import-export house," he said, serious for once.

"Where's one of those?"

"In St. Louis," he replied. Disappointed, I stared blankly at him and sighed.

Instead Jack and I moved to Elsberry, a small eastern Missouri town, too far away for us to afford the daily round trip to St. Louis. I took a job as a part-time waitress and contemplated the two-room hired hand's quarters we had rented in the country to save money. It was on the edge of the landlord's property. Its four corners rested on boulders just high enough off the ground to provide a haven for groundhogs. It was clean and neat, but it had no plumbing, no toilet, and no running water. The cistern had worms in it. The outhouse, built inside an old chicken coop, had a yellow-jacket nest in it within twenty inches of our rear ends. That winter it snowed eighteen inches, and we had to shovel our way to it.

To hide our dirty clothes, we tacked a curtain around a small table used as a kitchen counter, but that didn't fool our Labrador retriever. One day she waited until we went to the store before starting to empty the laundry basket and carrying its entire contents, piece by piece, out the poorly hung screen door. When we came home, the landlord was standing on his front porch laughing. He pointed to a blouse in the junipers, a washcloth stuck to tree bark, and a pair of jeans lying on the front stoop, with one leg contorted to the north and the other headed west.

Part of our rent reduction hinged on feeding the landlord's horse during the months he wintered in Florida. I knew nothing about farm animals, except which end the food went in and which end it came out. I had no clue that a horse wasn't dying when he lay on his back like an upturned cockroach, writhing and grunting. I also thought baby pigs were to be picked up and petted.

One night around midnight, a rat got into the kitchen. In a dazed half-sleep, Jack got up to shoot him, but I convinced him the landlord wouldn't take kindly to bullet holes in his floor. Then a groundhog tried to eat the underneath part of our house. Jack waited for days for him to come out so he could kill him and finally blew off his head one sub-freezing morning. The dog didn't even want the remains. The groundhog's frozen, cleanly decapitated carcass laid in state, until we finally threw it over the fence to the pigs.

Shooting a groundhog soon moved into another type of warfare that Jack had long been dreading. No matter how many ploys he attempted to try to escape the military, it finally caught up with him, and they called him up to serve his six months in the Army. That meant I needed to find a job, so the best thing for me to do was to leave our furniture in Elsberry and temporarily move back in with my parents. I had no idea what would be in store for me.

Around 1960. Left to right, front: Edward Lowrance, Elizabeth Lowrance
Back: Grandma Edith Lowrance, Janet Lowrance, Ann Hamilton, Jack Hamilton

Chapter 6

I SHOULD HAVE KNOWN BETTER

While Jack was shooting off guns at Army basic training, I landed a job in Columbia as a floral designer. I was glad I had taken that class at MU. I could at least pronounce all the tropical plant names. I was decorating a wedding reception table, when a Neosho, Missouri, speech teacher and I struck up a conversation. When he found out I was a Spanish graduate, he told me his high school needed a Spanish teacher.

I quivered. A real job, doing something I swore I would never do. I was an idiot, because I hadn't even taken any education courses, but I got the job on the promise that I could get the minimum in summer school right before school started.

So in 1961, we moved into a pink house across from the railroad tracks in a neighborhood full of retirees. Edith and her husband lived across the street. She was a nurse, and they lived in a fourteen room house that could have passed for a nursing home.

On a cool fall day, she finally found time to clean the dog dribbles, fingerprints, food, and insect remains from the inside of all those windows. Her neighbor came over to inspect and started griping at her for not washing them on the outside. Edith glared at her for a moment and said, "Shoot, I washed them on the inside so I could see out. If you want to see in, *you* can wash them on the outside!" Edith didn't like the neighbor lady anyway, because she put knit booties on her little dog's feet to keep the chiggers off when he went outside.

Edith maintained the same careless stance when it came to planting their garden. She claimed her husband did everything by the book and his plants all died. "Crap! I dig a hole, plop in a plant, stomp it down, water it, and say 'Grow, dang-it!' Mine all live."

An older couple named Griffin lived next door and ran a laundry in their walk-in basement. I got careless about collecting up some of our laundry from under the bed without checking first, and was totally embarrassed when three prophylactics went through the wringer and went off like bombs. Mrs. Griffin said, "You two need a rest."

Polly was living with us for the time being and fell in love with Ward Griffin. To him he must have looked like Grandpa, as Polly wasn't prone to taking up with strangers. In fact, a month after we moved in, an irate salesman came to the door, verbally scorching us for two days of laughing at him from inside the living room instead of answering the doorbell. We figured if Polly could get rid of a salesman, we'd be sure and leave his drapes open so he could laugh at anyone he wanted to.

By then we also had a different dog, a part Labrador retriever and part curb setter named Spook, because she had white feet that practically glowed in the dark. She wasn't too happy the day we brought home a baby skunk that some country kids saved after its mother got killed. I had always wanted one, and an ad had appeared in the paper, placed by a couple trying to find homes for five of them. It only took three hours to potty-train it on a newspaper, and when we weren't looking, it went out on the back porch and helped itself to a soft bed made out of a piece of Spook's backside. The dog didn't take kindly to a skunk running up and down her back, and the next thing we knew they were both out in the yard playing Who's the Boss. The skunk won and perfumed up both the yard and the Griffin's barbeque, which didn't sit well with them for the next twenty-four hours.

We took the skunk to a vet to get her de-fumed, but she died in the process, and we had to order another one from a fur farm. The delivery man held its cage out so far in front of him, that he almost tripped over a rock and sped off in his delivery truck like his tailpipe was on fire. Later we regretted that we had bought a skunk and paid good money for the worms that went with it, so we decided to wait until the next spring when we could get a real skunk again out of the woods.

Luckily some friends had a pet skunk that had been fooling around with a wild male, netting three babies born under the house, who became nosey little house guests. We were offered two of them, half-grown and still armed. Gratefully we told our friends we would even be glad to pay for the de-fuming of the one they wanted to keep.

Instead of caging all three of them, it was safer to turn them loose in the house until the morning trip to the vet. After a night of playing in the cupboards, they took refuge under the kitchen stove, where I had to gently pull them out by their tails, carefully tuck their tails under them, and deposit them in a chicken-wire cage in the back of the station wagon. We thought stares from passing motorists gawking at the parrot were funny, but the vision of three skunks bordered on traffic mayhem.

When we finally got to Joplin, the temperature was beginning to escalate, and the vet decided to put the cage outside under a tree in the yard by his office until he could get to them. While he was busy elsewhere, the skunks reached through the chicken wire and dug up around the cage, dragging cool clumps of dirt and grass into it, thus tearing up his yard. When we came to pick them up, he was not happy. Not only did he have an ugly grassless rectangle in his yard, but he had already had a bit too much to drink. That didn't stop him from operating on the skunks, though, which was a big mistake for him. Half-grown skunks have scent glands as large as those of full grown ones. A partially inebriated vet trying to remove six of them had obviously not been a pretty sight.

High school finally started, and my first year of teaching was about as good or bad as anyone else's. I had large classes, as many were encouraged to take a foreign language due to the Sputnik scare. In spite of too much paper-grading, I loved the language and had a great bunch of students.

When I got a bit behind grading papers, I invited the Spanish II students to the house on Saturdays to help me grade Spanish I papers. There were two rewards; all the potato chips, cookies, and Cokes they could consume, and the chance to be with other Spanish students of the opposite sex whom they secretly admired. Little did they know they were also being tricked into mastery learning.

When the students heard about Polly, they begged me to bring him to school, and I finally got permission. They were warned he could bite, and they held perfectly still while he walked pigeon-toed up and down the aisles. They almost became petrified, when he started climbing up the chair and onto the shoulder of a boy on the back row. I waited for a puddle to show up under someone's chair, but all Polly did was sing in the boy's ear and nibble on his collar.

One student decided he would give me the final test of courage and came in after lunch cradling something in his hands. He gently turned a pink-eyed white mouse into my hands that he'd filched from the biology lab. The mouse was totally tame, so after I petted him for a couple of minutes, I gave him back to the kid. He had to corral the squirmy thing in his pocket for the next forty-five minutes, which was not an easy thing, as he had a hole in it and it got loose once in his pants.

The day after the last day of school, we woke up to a sign in the yard saying, "Fresh Catfish Served Here" and exactly 100 beer cans in our yard, which I had a hunch were terms of endearment. Sure enough, three of my favorite male students showed up later, proud of having stayed up nights collecting and emptying them by the side of the road, at great risk of having their hides flattened by trucks. As a reward, I sat them down in front of a table of cookies and soda pop and taught them everything we knew about decorating newlyweds' cars and apartments. When our first baby came in November, the same three came to my hospital room, bringing their good wishes and gifts of baby clothes.

My job as full time teacher came to a temporary end after one year because of the pregnancy. Two months after our first boy, Scott, was born, we paid a sickly down payment for a small greenhouse in Joplin – the epitome of Jack's dream to be self-employed in the ornamental horticulture business.

Everything was there on one piece of property, which contained the greenhouse, a truck garage, a car garage, a chicken pen, the original little stone room where the former owners first grew African violets, a shed, and a home to live in. We were so busy the first three years, that it took us that long to discover there was an outhouse concealed in the back end of the shed. The house had been bought during WWII for forty-five dollars and moved across town to be set on the front part of the twenty acres that was now ours. We didn't know what to do with twenty acres outside the city limits and across from a golf course, but at least it had two or three sink holes in it where we could eventually deposit defunct appliances.

The trouble with having property off the beaten track was that it became a haven for after-dark neckers and drunks, who would usually park on the west side, where they thought they were hidden. When Janet came to visit, she started calling it the No Tell Motel. That was fine, until the drunks got a little loud. We finally managed to park our station wagon with the front pointing in that direction, so if we got tired of the noise, we could turn the headlights on them. That caught a few relieving themselves in the weeds and some others doing things not to be proud of.

One night a fellow drove out in his car to sober up, not even noticing how close to the house he was. Finally he'd had enough and threw up everything including his false teeth. That created enough ruckus to send Jack outside to see what the matter was. He offered the man a flashlight, but to no avail. Finally he brought him inside to see if he could sober him up with a few cups of coffee. Much later I learned from a medical journal, that coffee doesn't sober up anything; all you do is fill up a drunk with coffee. The man left the next morning, still without his teeth, which probably left him with a lot of explaining to do at home.

The greenhouse years began the era of Jack buying dilapidated vehicles to use as our second car. The first was a truck belonging to his brother, Ed, that wouldn't go into second gear unless you reached out the window and pulled a rope. The next was an old station wagon we only paid two hundred dollars for, that barely lurched me to work later when I got a real job. After putting new tires on it, we sold it and at least got our original two hundred dollars back. The last one came some years later. Since Jack drove it, somehow I missed ever getting in on the driver's side to notice that the front door looked like it had been eaten by a shark. I found out later, that when he bought it from a relative, it had been parked out in a field for quite some time. A horse had been eating hay out of the back end, and when they barely started up the engine, mice ran out from under the dashboard.

Nursing a baby in a greenhouse boiler room didn't exactly fit my dream of child-rearing. Earlier I had read Dr. Spock from cover to cover, since I had spent only three hours taking care of a baby in my whole life and I didn't want to make any stupid errors with Scott. Jack and I both had to work to make the baby thing go, so we took what came and set up the playpen in between the two greenhouse sections. Before it was all over, the playpen held two more children at one time or another.

Some customers were pretty funny. One lady came in with a toddler's pour-out potty pan instead of a flower pot. She had a friend in the hospital, who had just had a terrible hemorrhoid operation, and she wanted me to plant a long, cucumber-shaped, stickery cactus in it for him.

As long as he wouldn't bother the customers, we'd let Polly come down to the greenhouse with us on warm days so he could run up and down the steam pipes, his green feathers blending in with the plants. He could cry like the baby and laugh like a customer, so most of the time, no one was the wiser about his presence, unless he started doing target practice on the African violets. Once he got so loud, that a customer reported it sounded like someone back there was pulling arms and legs off the children.

We weren't making enough money with the greenhouse alone and eventually had to set up a flower shop in the front end. This was right down the alley from what I'd been doing as a florist in Columbia, but this time I got to be in on more of the action, especially with weddings and funerals. For weddings, I had to arrive an hour early, giving me ample time to enjoy all the free entertainment that came with them. Flower girls always seemed to get lost. I finally found one in the reception hall, with her finger in the punch, swirling frozen blobs around at breakneck speed. If not lost, they waited until halfway down the aisle to announce, "I gotta wee wee!"

Ring bearers stayed put and made bold announcements or sometimes big mistakes. "I'm the ring burier!" one told me. Another dropped the groom's ring down the furnace grating on his way down the aisle.

When it came to instructions, nervous grooms never were any good at remembering which of their hands were right or left. Sometimes ring bearers or flower girls had to remind them. One groom's buddies secretly put big letters L and R on the bottom of the groom's shoes, so that when he knelt at the altar, they were visible to the whole congregation. Ceremony was even further abandoned in one country church, where someone planned for candles, but no candle lighters. Two black-toothed ushers came up and lit them with their cigarette lighters.

Brides usually held their composure better than grooms. However, a fellow florist said she saw one bride start to cry halfway down the aisle. Her handkerchief had become lost in her dress, so she took off her glove and blew her nose on it.

Although weddings were joyous occasions, many of them were lit like funeral parlors. I guess there was supposed to be something romantic about turning out all the lights and basking in the glow of the candles. One poor minister practically had to climb the candelabrum to read the wedding vows, and the organist had to abandon her wedding music and play some show tunes that she knew by heart.

I thought I had just enough time to get through a wedding before our second son, David, would be due; however, this baby had plans and wasn't going to horse around getting here like Scott did. Two hours after sudden labor pains and a screeching ride to the Neosho hospital, out he popped. So two days after David was born, Jack loaded up flowers in the big ice chest and brought them to the hospital, where I had to make three bouquets, five corsages and five boutonnieres in my hospital bed, cheered on by nurses, curious patients, and bedpan ladies. I knew very soon that Jack and I were going to have a "Come to Jesus" talk about him learning how to make corsages and wedding stuff.

Funerals were a little more spur-of-the-moment than weddings, but still likely to keep us up half the night working. There was nothing predictable about them either. When the neighbor lady living at the bottom of the hill died, her husband asked me to make her a corsage. Just as I was ready to pin it on her in the casket, the mortician leaped from behind the drapes and blurted, "Don't stick her!" An inner voice told me to take pictures of her before I left and not to tell her poverty-stricken husband just yet. Months later, he came to the greenhouse to talk, lamenting that in all their years together, he had never had a picture of her.

"She was never more beautiful than when she was in that casket, wearing your pretty corsage," he said, tears streaming down his unshaven face. Quietly I told him what I had done and asked him if he wanted to see the pictures. He nodded and cried the whole time he was picking one out. I framed his favorite, which he put on his dresser as if she were his new bride.

I wondered if I would ever be asked by a family to photograph a corpse, and finally I was. Since corpses couldn't pose, it was all up to me. Should I tweak the hair a little to get rid of facial lines? Mother had always taught me to get rid of distracting background things, like crooked wall lines and plants that looked like they were growing out of people's heads. How could I get a good face-on without crawling on top of the casket? I remembered the time I couldn't get a good, straight picture of a half-concealed school, without having to lie on top of a dog house across the street.

It was always good to get away from the greenhouse on Wednesday nights and Sundays and drive back to Neosho and work with our two choirs. I had no people skills for the volunteer junior choir, including kids from grades four through eight, so I had to contrive my own system of rewards and punishment.

I quickly learned that with the exception of eighth graders, boys and girls treated each other like lepers. So punishment for mischief meant making boys and girls sit next to each other. The reward for good behavior at the end of the rehearsals was getting to sing silly songs like "Dirty Lil," which went:

"Dirty Lil, Dirty Lil
Lived on top a garbage hill.
Never took a bath and never will,
(Cough, spit), Dirty Lil."

Of course I had learned songs like this while in high school from ministers at church camp, so that made them acceptable. Another favorite was a rendition of "My Bonnie Lies Over the Ocean," which started out,

"My Bonnie has tuberculosis.
My Bonnie has only one lung....

The very favorite was "The Billboard Song," which I found on a piece of mimeographed paper in the music closet. It was still remembered by four of them forty years later at the church's anniversary celebration.

The only junior choir kid I had trouble approaching was the monotone. Ordinarily monotones got drowned out by the others, but this kid was super-nice, loud, loved the choir and the Lord, and never missed a rehearsal or performance. I couldn't hide him, because he had bright red hair and was six inches taller than anyone else. Finally, when the others said, "He's not singing the same song we are," enough times, he stayed home.

About this time, when I was battling monotones and young adolescent girls, I thought about Janet having a gay old time overseas playing with the London Symphony during the summer. She was lucky that she played the flute, as her cello-playing friend was having to pay half fare to get his oversized instrument a seat on the plane back home. But later, she told me that they ran into an unsuspecting lady at the ticket counter, who asked the cellist, "And what instrument is that?"

"It's a flute," he replied.

She pored over a list, running her finger down the page.

"OK. A flute. You can go on."

With a baby coming soon, I was beginning to look about like that cello. When the choir first learned I was going to have a baby, they were excited. I got five offers to baby-sit after junior choir, while I sang with the adult choir. When I announced November 11 as the due date, unknown to me, one girl thought that was the Gospel. When I appeared at church November 11 to direct them, she quivered during the entire service, fearful I would have it in the pew. I found out later that she wasn't the only one.

I thought I would never quit having children and would be forced to wear space suits forever. Even with a new church and a new adult choir, I was still clad in maternity wear. In the middle of a rehearsal, the choir suddenly burst out laughing.

"Are you planning on growing wings?" an alto asked.

"Why?"

"Look behind you!" I had put my maternity top on backwards, with the pointy darts over my shoulder blades instead of over my boobs.

Luckily Dennis, the boy that was supposed to be a girl after having two boys, was born without incident. With his arrival, I had proudly set a record – one baby late, one early, one on time, and all by natural childbirth. There had been some doubt about Dennis, as when we went to the Neosho hospital, our doctor said I wasn't ready yet. I knew I was and wasn't about to start back to Joplin and have him in the van.

"Why don't you go downtown to the sidewalk sale and walk around for awhile and try not to have it on the cement," the doctor suggested. I tried to hide in between racks of clothes waving in the streets so I wouldn't have to answer any more questions from friends asking what I was doing there instead of home working in the greenhouse.

My doubts about raising children in a greenhouse had been confirmed a couple of years earlier the day I saw an unidentified snake headed for the dark underneath side of the playpen with Scott in it. I was over eight months pregnant with David, and had visions of the snake being poisonous and killing more than one of us. All I could find to kill him with were a rag and a telephone book, until I stumbled upon some hedge shears. Irrationally, I tried to cut him in half. Then I realized that with my poor aim and my stupidity, he could bite me. Before he could muster a strike, I whacked him behind the head. I nervously made four inch segments out of the rest of him to make sure he was dead. I gathered up Scott and headed for the house, waiting for Jack to get back from late deliveries. Sure enough it was a copperhead.

If I had known for sure he wasn't poisonous, I would have picked him up or gently shoo'd him out like I sometimes did when blacksnakes came calling at the house. A big one came in one day, when our friend Brenda was there, and crawled under the desk in the spare bedroom. Brenda didn't want to go in there for weeks afterwards, feeling he might still be hiding. One morning I happened to glance up at the top edge of the shower stall to see a snakeskin draped over it. I knew I took pretty hot showers, but didn't know one would make a snake want to shed his skin.

Our old house had some other problems. We noticed that mouse holes had been nailed shut with the round pieces cut from orange juice cans, then painted over. I couldn't see any more holes, but one mouse got in that got so tame, she would sit in the middle of the living room floor and wash her face in front of us. She eluded every attempt to catch her, but I eventually found out where she was hiding, along with some of her girlfriends.

I had just put some dry dog food in the bottom of a medium-sized waste can on the back porch and had shoved Scott's little red stool up next to it to make more room on the porch. The next morning, when I started out to feed the dog, I looked in the waste can, and fourteen baby mice were standing up on their hind legs waving their paws at me. They had evidently jumped from the stool into the waste can and then couldn't get back out. What a neat idea for a mousetrap, I thought. I knew if I turned them loose outdoors, they would all be back in to play within a week. Feeling bad about killing anything, I ultimately decided to flush them. This was going to be no small feat, with fourteen of them and accompanying dog food, without some of them possibly escaping and running up my arm, or me putting the whole plumbing system in distress.

Most of the rest of the wildlife on our property was harmless; consequently, in the spirit of my heritage, I taught the boys how to catch lizards and warm them up on their arms so they could pet them. The youngest one thought he had one and went to show it to a customer.

"See my wizard, wady?" he asked, as he handed her a scorpion he was holding up by his tail.

Periodically we had to fumigate the greenhouse for pests. Even though we did it long after it had closed, we still put up a danger sign on every entrance. All it would take would be for some stupid burglar to break in, and we would be up to our necks in a murder case!

Polly and Ward Griffin

Chapter 7

STANDING ON THE TOILET AND OTHER ESCAPADES

The greenhouse wasn't making us a decent enough living, and it was time to do something about it. With a lady available part-time to help Jack, he hesitantly agreed I should see what kind of work I could find with the public schools. I hadn't taught school for five years and my two year temporary certificate in Spanish had expired. I even hoped for a substitute teaching job.

I dug the soil out of my fingernails, put on my best church dress, combed my hair, smeared on deodorant and some sweet-smelling perfume, and headed off for the Joplin Board of Education. After a thirty minute interview with the superintendent, with him doing most of the talking, he suddenly asked me if I would like to be a dean of girls at Joplin Senior High School. Shocked, I blurted out, "What does a dean of girls do?" He mentioned something about keeping the records for a thousand girls, checking to see who was skipping school, and looking after the girls in general. Finding out I typed twelve words a minute on a 1930 typewriter didn't faze him; there would be three student helpers every hour to take care of that. Unknown to me, the high school principal had been doing that job for three days and was full clear up to his ears with it. Anything with a teaching certificate, wearing a skirt, and smelling good would have been OK with him.

I went home and told Jack, who looked at me pensively. The next morning he quietly said, "Goodbye greenhouse lady." I felt sad for him and for the fact I was stepping out of his world to gradually find one of my own. I never forgot what he said; however, I knew I had to go.

The old station wagon jerked its way to the faculty parking lot, and I found my new office. I also found out what the superintendent hadn't told me about my job. There was no school nurse and two beds were in there. A thermometer was in a shoe box in a cabinet. The principal warmly greeted me, relieve that someone had been hired to handle girls' discipline. Girls' *what?* The bell had just rung, and they were swarming out there, spreading like some forest fire. I pretended everything was cool. I thought about the two meager hours of high school administration I had on my transcript.

Finally I sided up to the office girls each hour, and said, "OK, gals, clue me in on the routine here. What usually goes on in these beds?"

They snickered.

"That's for when someone is throwing up or something or has diarrhea, or maybe just pretending to be sick."

I found out later that no one knew how to spell that word. Excuse notes claimed dyurea, dirrea, diareeuh, and dyrreuh. Great, I thought. Now I can take the Bubonic plague home to my children.

This could be worse than substitute teaching, so the girls and I organized a posse. In time, they developed hand signals to alert me of known offenders. We logged in how many times a month someone came in complaining about her period or came in during the same hour. We kept each girl's excuses for being absent in a separate file and became handwriting experts. I got volunteers to help me nail neckers, smokers, and bathroom graffiti monsters. I told the girls to be clever and subtle and to use their best judgment in taking initiative.

I gave them fair warning. Anyone who ever lied to me or cheated at something would be banished from the team forever. That was all it took. They were excited and we were ready. With two really super assistant principals and a dean of boys to help us, how could we lose?

A couple of mornings later, just before the first bell, I got a phone call from one of the assistant principals. "Hamilton, we need you out in front of the building. There's a big crowd out there in front of the flagpole." I could tell he was trying not to laugh. I sauntered out, and sure enough, someone had taken down the American flag and run somebody's clothes up to the top. The crowd cheered. They quieted down as I studied the situation for a few seconds. Without a fuss, I calmly undid the rope and slowly lowered the garment back down. I detached the clothespin securing it to the rope and waved it over my head as I meandered back into the building. The crowd cheered again and went on to class.

My father had always taught me that if you don't make a big fuss over something like that, the evildoer might eventually hang himself. We had to wait six weeks before the culprit started bragging about it in class, and we nailed him.

Not long afterwards, a strange man in a suit came to my door and gazed at me for a few moments. He asked me if I were happy doing my job. I told him I loved it. He nodded, almost in disbelief, and left.

"Who was that?" I asked the girls.

"That was Jack Allman, the assistant superintendent of schools." I quickly jotted down "Jack Almond, Assistant Supt."

It took a bit before girls started pulling fast ones. Not knowing we were counting, one came in to lie down for the third time. The girls were primed.

"Honey," I said, "when someone comes in for the third time, we assume she really has something wrong with her and we have to take her temperature. Sally, would you get out that thermometer for me?" There was some shuffling around in the shoe box.

"Mrs. Hamilton, did you know that the only thermometer we have is a rectal one?"

"I'm afraid so. I'll take it down to the bathroom to make sure it's been cleaned up." That gave the girl on the bed time to disappear and never return.

One girl, who hadn't been warned by the others, came in once too often. The local mortician's daughter was on duty that hour.

I happened to look around and see her fixing up the corpse on the bed, folding her hands across her abdomen and starting to put makeup on her with a brush. She did it with such a straight face that I had to turn around and look out the window so she wouldn't see me laughing. When I turned back around, the corpse had left.

We had one young lady who didn't like her fourth hour home economics class she had right after lunch. She marched in for about the fourth time and announced that she had eaten a bug and was sick.

"How did you know you ate it?" I asked.

"I saw it on my fork on my bite of spaghetti and I *ate* it!" she sniveled. I looked at her for awhile. I shouldn't have said this.

"Do you feel it crawling around in there?" That was her last time too.

One week, the girls had been noticing a couple kissing outside the classroom next door until after the tardy bell rang, and then darting into class late. When the teacher finally reported it, I asked the girls, "Who wants this one?"

Sara piped up, "I do, but I don't know what to do." I knew she wouldn't crack a smile, so I took her aside, got her a pad of paper and a pencil, and wrote her a pass to get out of class two minutes earlier the hour before. She was primed to stare incessantly at the couple, moving around them to get the best view. If that didn't work, the next step was to take notes. The next day, the couple was not there. The third day, I sent the girls out to find their new hiding place, but they never found one.

If mischief wasn't happening in the halls, it was likely to be going on in study hall. One teacher was having trouble determining the source of muffled frog noises coming from the back of the room. He was fairly certain who was doing it, but couldn't quite prove it, so he said to the suspected perpetrator, "I need your help. Someone back here is making frog noises, and I'm going to put you in charge of finding out who it is."

"Whattya gonna do if you catch him?"

"I'm going to kick the crap out of him."

The frog noises ceased after that. It left me with a strategy that I used for years afterwards. Find the one you think is the culprit and put him or her in charge of finding the culprit. It worked every time, and I didn't have to threaten anything.

Skipping school was another form of recreation. The school system was already ahead of the game with its own truant officer, who had previously been an elementary principal. He knew which alleys and garbage cans the students were hiding in and with whom. If they continued to skip school after he caught them, my next step was to call the woman truant officer downtown, who had a voice like a man's. When she got on the phone with the parents to remind them about the law concerning fines and jail sentences for parents who couldn't keep their kids in school, truants started appearing out of nowhere.

In some ways, I wasn't prepared for this job. Although married and with three small children, I had been sheltered at home growing up. Consequently I was unprepared when a business teacher came downstairs to talk to me about one of her students. It seemed the young lady had felt something was not right at home and had come to church one night and confessed the whole thing in front of the congregation. The teacher said it was incest.

"What's incest?" I asked her. At that point, I began my short course in Dysfunction 101. I knew it was time to quit taking girls down to the bathroom so they could tell me all kinds of private things away from the ears of the office girls. I needed to talk to Jack Allman, alias Almond, the assistant superintendent.

I needed to know more about him anyway. We met in the school cafeteria one day to have coffee and talk about girls' issues and size each other up. We talked for a long time, and I wondered to myself where all the nice men like him had been when I was of marriageable age.

On a whim, I asked him how old he was. He said forty. I was twenty-nine. Heck, he would have been too old. I drank some more coffee and continued my wishful thinking anyway.

Jack turned out to be my biggest supporter. We were already in a strange situation, as the usual line and staff procedure had been changed in relation to who would punish girls for major misdeeds. By prior arrangement, I was handling ninety-nine percent of the girls' discipline on campus. The about-to-retire principal had enough other worries on his hands. So when it came time to suspend a girl, she went directly to the assistant superintendent instead of the principal. That system was highly unusual, but it worked.

As far as girls' personal problems were concerned, I was already asking for help from the counselors, who were very gracious in their approval of what I was already doing. It was teamwork effort beyond my wildest dreams.

Next I made an appeal for an inner office within our larger room. It met with administrative approval, and it wasn't long before the carpenters came and the inner office was finished. At least the girls had someplace to go where they could tell their stories behind closed doors and drapes. Even the principal had a place to hide for a few minutes when he'd had enough. I would either stay and let him talk it out, or would ask if he wanted me to leave and hang a "Quarantine" sign on the door before I left.

The inner office was a blessing. One day I stood in front of the mirror, asking myself, "Ann, is this really you, untrained half-counselor, half-administrator loving what you're doing and having fun at the same time?" I knew at that point I had to go back to graduate school, but to study what? The training programs for these two professions were very different, and my colleagues claimed I needed to choose one or the other. That was not how I was cut out.

After a summer full of education courses to revive my teaching certificate, and a first semester evening counseling course to see how I would fare with that, I went at it again. The high school had become so crowded that it was time to do something about it. Our building was renamed Parkwood, and a new one named Memorial was created using the building once inhabited by Joplin Junior College. Before my second year began, there was also a shift in administration. One of our teachers was hired for the position of dean of boys to finish out his last year before retirement. He took to it well, but didn't have a clue as to what he was supposed to do at the first school dance. I suggested we go in there and patrol, look sinister, and watch for the usual kissing and smoking. He looked so perplexed when he emerged from all the squirmy dancing and loud music.

"When I was a young man and a boy acted like that in front of a girl, we gave him worm medicine!" he said.

Jack Allman dropped by that night to see how we were doing. I told him what our colleague had said, which prompted him to do some unholy dance imitations that threw his back out. It was like what one of our other colleagues used to do, when he tried to imitate a fat lady in a girdle trying to walk.

We targeted the restrooms again, where the fire dragons lived. We actually had to see them smoking before we could punish them. I knew all my shoes had been memorized, so I had to lock my stall door and stand on the toilet to see any smoking going on in the next stall. As soon as they found out what I was doing, they moved to the space between the last stall and the wall. Forgetting their physics, they didn't realize I could peer through the crack in the door and see them at right angles in the mirror.

I was comparing notes with an administrator from another school, who had his own favorite spot in the boys' bathroom. He had finally asked himself, "What am I doing here, an educated man, standing on top of an orange crate in a broom closet in the boys' bathroom, looking through a knothole?"

I made a haul on one of my regular restroom trips and brought out a shoe box I found on the window ledge. It contained a bra and panties. One of the administrators should have known better than to ask me what was in it. I took off the lid right out there in the hall, with students passing by. Red-faced, he asked, "What are you going to do with that?"

"Put it in the lost and found right next to your office."

The principal types were way too happy to have a female administrator around, especially when it came to enforcing the dress code and measuring skirts. One of them even called me once to tell me there was a forty-year-old maxi-mamma wearing a mini-skirt outside his door, and would I please come get her.

A dilemma came when one of my office girls wanted to turn in her sister for rolling her skirt up to the bottom of her rump and trying to hide from me, but she didn't want to rat on her sister and get caught. I thought for a moment and said, "Well, I'll bet if a typed anonymous note appeared on my desk in the next twenty minutes while I'm down the hall, it would give me something to show her while she's hiding from me in the lunch line."

The anonymous note system worked for almost anything. For example, girls could secretly report fights that were going to happen. Girls' fights were always on time, at the designated place, and with a selected cast of characters including the Bullies and the Pickables. The Pickables were usually sweet and fat and not prone to defending themselves, and the Bullies could raze whole buildings. If the fight were to be off-campus, I could call the city juvenile officer, who would get into his Clark Kent clothes and sneak up on them in his old truck. That didn't fool any of them, but they would scatter like chickens anyway.

Girls' fights were dirty. I thought about just letting them kill each other and collecting up the hair and putting it in an envelope later to add to my collection. Girls didn't always fight girls. I was meandering down the hall, when I noticed a large, black girl about to slug a black fellow half her size. Quietly I came up to her with a big smile and said, "Hey - you're just the gal I need to see! I've got something really funny to tell you." I waved her away from the scene, and as we were strolling down the hall, far from the crowd, I asked, "Do you know what I just got you out of?"

Only once did we have a new girl come to work for us in the middle of the year. We waited until she got to know us before we gave her the unexpected initiation ceremony. I scribbled out a note and told her to take it to room such-and-such upstairs, and to knock on the door fairly loudly since the teacher didn't hear well and always kept it shut. It was an unmarked boy's bathroom. She came back red-faced and giggling, saying, "You all played a trick on me!"

One day we got an extra office girl because of some new program. Her name was Margaret and she had B.O. The girls and I talked at length about how to handle it, but we all balked at how to do it. We thought one of the P.E. teachers would fix it for us, but unfortunately, the stench was in all of her clothes.

"You'd think she'd never get a boyfriend smelling like that," I said.

"She has a boyfriend," said one of them.

"How does he stand it then?" I asked.

"He's a garbage man," she answered. "After smelling what he has to every day, she probably smells pretty good to him."

I gave up. After four days, I found her P.E. teacher and started begging. "Don't worry," she said. "I'll just go up to her and tell her she stinks." That didn't work either, and we finally had to ask the program director to find her another position.

Margaret wasn't the only disrupting odor. The biology classes were into dissecting. Most kids thought frogs were bad enough, but these students were into baby sharks. Band members nearby were gagging over their music and home economics girls' eyes were watering. I took this one on myself. I bought a can of sickening sweet lilac air spray and sneaked up to their door. With only my arm showing, I reached in and gave them a fifteen second blast. The laughter soon died down, and eventually the smell did too. Maybe they took it outdoors.

From time to time, individual students went to great lengths to make their marks. My biggest problem was a girl named Tammy, who rode on a broom. She had already spread the rumor that students could see my underwear reflected from my patent leather shoes. I was willing to try anything. On a hunch, I confined her to a lonely desk in my office until she could behave. The girls were instructed to be kind to her when she behaved herself and to ignore her when she didn't. I gave her a limit of three days to turn herself around before threatening her with a worse kind of purgatory. She blubbered and squirmed around a bit, looking for something to use to disrupt. Finally she said, "Mrs. Hamilton, there's a big black spider crawling up the wall behind me." Sure enough, he was a dandy.

"He won't eat much," I told her.

"But he might bite me!" she squealed.

"I'm sure he doesn't like your looks any better than you like his. If he gets too close, let me know and I'll get him." She got real quiet after that.

I didn't have to keep her for three days. After a day, she had enough of us and was very little trouble after that. I told the story to Jack Allman, asking him if there weren't some similar way we could control discipline problems. He responded that he and some of his colleagues had already gotten wind of this kind of approach, calling it in-school suspension.

It wasn't long before he had the concept in place, a room set aside, and a teacher hired. Right away our troubles started to diminish. It made sense. After all, when a student skipped school, it gave him a chance to go home, put his feet up on the coffee table, and eat popcorn. After he had done it enough times, he would get suspended and go home to the same scenario, this time with a TV series. With in-school suspension, he had to stay at school and do homework the whole time, which was equated with a jail sentence. He couldn't even go to the bathroom without going with the whole crowd. That was the pits, and he never wanted to do it again.

I was warned by an assistant principal that some parents would attempt to unlawfully claim custody of their children and try to come to school to get them. Luckily one of these called in advance, giving us time to get his kid out of class and hide her, terrified, in a closet.

Some cases of abuse came as a surprise to me, as I often knew the parents as greenhouse customers and respected community leaders. A mother and daughter both came to school one morning in tears, with facial and arm bruises. The father had thrown his daughter against the wall for spilling a little garbage she was trying to carry out. His wife had strands of her own hair she could pull out as a result of him grabbing her and throwing her around when she tried to defend the girl.

Some students would actually flee from home. Then there were boys who disappeared with girls. When Kyle and his girlfriend showed up missing, one of the office girls said,

"That Kyle, he's so dumb!"

"He's not dumb anymore," said another one.

"No, I mean he's just plain dumb. He used to paint sideburns on his face with black shoe polish, until one day he got to sweating during football practice, and his sideburns dribbled down into his shirt."

One day, while I was taking a break in the faculty lounge, a teacher asked me, "Why is it, with the kind of job you have, you are always so happy and never get mad?"

"There's really nothing to get mad about," I said. "These are basically good kids who just need to be outsmarted. It's their problems, not mine – they just need their tails twisted a little."

In due time, they all got their laughs at my expense. Not wanting to be driving the town slum car, I got up early to take it to the car wash before work. I opened the window, put in my change, and drove in. After the car and I both got washed, I closed the window and had to go home and dry my hair and change clothes. I called in that I would be late. By the time I got to work, the office girls and any handy teachers had been instructed to spread the news like wildfire. Almost forty years later, people still reminded me of it.

I wasn't the only one targeted for fame. As I wandered into the main office early one afternoon, the administrators were huddled together, convulsed in laughter. "Hamilton, you should have been there!" one of them said.

"Where?"

"At the administrator's luncheon yesterday."

"What happened?" I asked.

"Allman decided to give up smoking and to take up chewing. After dessert, he put a wad in his mouth and then didn't know what to do with it after he got into chewing. It was really a boring speaker we had anyway, and pretty soon Allman figured no one would notice if he used his paper cup to spit in and keep it hidden between his legs."

Another one piped up. "Every time he got ready to spit, he hunched over below the tablecloth, spit in the cup, and then rolled his eyes and grinned at all the people on each side of him. That got the whole bunch to laughing, and the poor speaker couldn't figure out what he'd said that was so funny!"

There was nothing funny about what was going to happen next. My husband had gotten an offer to take over a greenhouse in Columbia. It was going to be a nice move for him, but not for me, as I loved my job. The last thing I wanted to do was to leave it, especially in the middle of the school year, as they wanted Jack to take over in January. We agreed that I would have to return to the greenhouse to run it until it could be sold, and that if needed, the children and I would stay with the new owners for a month to help them with the transition.

I told the administration and then the office girls and started looking over the current staff to see if there were someone special who might like my job. The obvious candidate was the biology teacher, who not only had a wonderful sense of humor, but who seemed to know which punishment fit which offense. I remembered the time a boy in her class stung a girl on the arm with a carefully-aimed rubber band. Feeling an eye for an eye and a tooth for a tooth was merited, she let the girl sit behind the boy for the rest of the hour, poised with her own rubber band. She let him have it behind his ear just as the bell rang.

A few days before I was to leave, three office girls showed up at my house unexpectedly late one afternoon, bringing our babysitter with them. I knew they were up to something, but let them blindfold me and lead me to a waiting car. We ended up at the home of one of them, where twenty were waiting with a big surprise party and a nice gift. They paid me one of the nicest compliments I had ever gotten.

"You never let us get away with anything, but you were always so nice about it."

The day came for me to say goodbye, and I could hardly do it. I packed up what few things I had in my office and slowly went around touching bases with so many I had learned to love. I picked a time when I knew my closest colleagues would be occupied and found my way to the parking lot for the last time. I felt like I was drowning in my tears. Little did I know, that decades later, this high school that had changed my whole life would be destroyed by the Joplin EF5 tornado of May 22, 2011.

Jack Allman

Chapter 8

STUDYING TO DO WHAT?

The greenhouse sold and was finally out of my hair. So were the aphids, snakes, mice, and hornets. In August of 1969, the boys and I moved into the vermin-free new house Jack had purchased for us. A bookkeeping job was waiting for me there in the greenhouse, which would make our income adequate enough for me to start graduate school. I would be trapped for awhile, but on my way to finding an occupation where I could hopefully make a difference again.

My mother caught wind of the graduate school business and told one of her friends I was fifty years ahead of my time. I couldn't remember whether that meant I resembled a hairy-legged pioneer woman or someone wanting to ride around in a rocket. I soon found out when I walked into Dr. Neil Aslin's office. I wanted to see if I qualified to start on MU's master's program in secondary school administration.

"Welcome! You're my first woman advisee," he said, and shook my hand.

Dr. Aslin had known me all through junior high and high school, when he was the Columbia superintendent of schools and his son, Jack, was in my graduating class. I pondered over the women who thought they had to wave bras on sticks in the air to get equality, when all I had to do was to walk into the office of a colleague and ask. I found out that administrators just wanted a sincere and willing woman to join them in their effort to have school.

I could imagine my mother thinking that women shouldn't aspire to high school administrative jobs. Who would want to chase after students skipping school, smuggling pizzas into the classroom, and all kinds of other things? What did she think I had just been doing in Joplin?

In this Age of Studied Tackiness, my classmates studying to be high school principals would look at me and say, "Gee, it's sure nice to see something in a frilly blouse for a change." When they found out I had already been a dean of girls, they got real interested and turned loose a parade of questions.

What is a principal to do when a girl comes into his office, closes the door, opens her blouse and then yells, "He fondled me!" How do you get some women teachers to patrol the girls' restrooms? How do you separate two girls fighting without getting accused of something? A couple of years later, I offered to do a segment at the annual meeting of the Missouri Association of Secondary School Principals on how to deal with girls' discipline problems and live to tell about it. A hundred men came.

I attended these meetings, mostly to keep my contacts while I was going to school. Since no other women, except maybe nuns, came to them, I was often mistaken for someone's wife and misdirected toward some shopping tour or to an afternoon on the golf course. However, the men treated me as an equal and with respect, except for one whose eyebrows met in the middle and who had some drops of drool in the corner of his mouth. He wanted to lead me into a dark corner of the dining room and "talk about school." I flipped on a light, and after an hour, he complained, "Don't you ever talk about anything except school?"

Administrative banquet meetings there brought on a new wrinkle, with either a fork or a spoon lying horizontally at the top of the plate. Not even I, the graduate of finishing school, knew what they were for. So we started placing bets.

"I think it's to flick food at the other table."

"I think it's a trap, and they're going to give us a test on it."

"It's a spare in case you drop something."

"No, it's to fish flies out of your water," someone said, as he looked down onto his with one eye.

That didn't seem to disturb the speaker, who was trying to tell us how people didn't touch or even look at each other anymore and how we should help change that.

"What do people do when they meet someone on the sidewalk? They look down or look to the right. And after they get into an elevator? They turn around and look at the doors. What do you think would happen if you turned around and smiled and looked at all the people after the doors closed? Men would start checking their fly fronts. Women would slyly feel for something unbuttoned. Tongues would search for stray spinach on the teeth. Combs would pop out, and everyone would get out on the next floor. Why don't you guys pat a student on the shoulder once in awhile or smile at a stranger on the sidewalk? It might be the only smile he or she has gotten in a week."

After two years, my master's degree in secondary school administration was finished. At the end of the spring semester of 1971, I stood up with the College of Education that had been herded into its section in the stadium, to receive my acknowledgements thereto and heretofore. A bit later, I felt a huge sense of freedom when I finally was able to get ahold of my diploma.

Almost immediately, I went back to my alma mater in search of a job. According to them, it had been renamed Columbia College "for fear the name Christian College might scare away some of the good customers." It now had male students. I was pleased that Elizabeth Kirkman was still there as dean of students. She was witty and competent, and no one dared pull the wool over her eyes. She needed an assistant, and after first refusing the low salary, I was called back by the president with a respectable figure and hired. I was now in for the dorm life routine.

Her pet peeve was one of the dorms that had been converted to co-ed, with the men housed on the lower floor. The men's floor was halfway underground, with the top half of the windows visible, and a cement moat surrounding the whole thing. With very little effort, a boy could crawl out of his window and into that of a girl's up above and get lost until before dawn.

In front of everyone at an administrator's meeting, she told the president, "I have a requisition for you. I want that moat filled up with water, and here's the paperwork for six alligators from Florida to be put in it."

There was no comparison between the fifties, sixties and now the seventies. I learned how to do dormitory drug raids. I had to buy a bigger purse so I could carry burglar tools. My green Datsun station wagon blended in with the vegetation so I could use it as a hideout for watching for drug drops. I had to deal with one student who was turned in for setting her shower curtain on fire while drunk. Another for taking drugs, her ashen lips and face trying to deny it.

I even inherited the Introduction to Education class. The College was moving into becoming a four-year institution, and I was to work out plans with Jefferson City for putting together a four- year education department. I required my students to buy a little book called *The Angel Inside Went Sour* before heading them out to observe local classrooms. They questioned why they should have to read about delinquent city kids moved to a special school in New York. However, they took a different view after they got back from observations. "All it takes is one of them in a classroom, and if you don't know what to do, you're dead," one commented.

Then I began my dress for success speech. "But I don't even own a dress!" one cried.

"Borrow," I said. "If in doubt, ask the principal what you should wear. Don't go for anything less than slacks and a nice blouse. Remember, I'm the only education teacher here who can recommend you, so until we get this program going, you're stuck with me."

After all, I hadn't gotten this job dressed up in my picnic clothes. I even suggested they dress up on airplanes and public transportation because it would make them look important and like they were in control.

Jack and I were driving to St. Louis, when we spied one of them hitchhiking along the highway. It was sweltering, but he was all dressed up in his white shirt, brown suit, and unpolished shoes. His long hair was carefully controlled with an elastic headband fashioned from the cutoff waistband of some white knit under-shorts. The words "J.C. Penney" were carefully centered across his forehead. Months later, the administration asked him to leave school.

This was an era when almost any kind of a bumper sticker could be found on a car. Buses even had to be painted. I eyed an old school bus on back campus that still ran. I appealed to Sid Larson, the art teacher, about letting some students turn it into a work of art. Perhaps he thought about the charcoal drawing I had made of his smashed-in fender a few years ago. He smiled. "If anything gets painted on it that shouldn't be there, I will paint a stripe down the inside of you."

The student helpers in my office were about as uninhibited, and had way too much fun at my expense. One day I had just poured myself a cup of coffee, when I had to go down the hall for a minute.

"What do you want in your coffee?" one of them asked.

"Everything. Sugar, cream, catsup, mustard."

When I got back, it took me a minute to figure out the taste of chicken bullion mixed in.

It was too much to move straight into doctoral studies without taking a semester off. Classes soon started up again, and I was beginning to get a taste of the future, when a fellow student came into the office muttering, "When spring comes, remember that thou shalt not beat thy advisor at golf right before doctoral exams."

Questions were pouring in from students already in administration and from would-be's. A nun from a parochial school asked how in the world were they to get funding in this era of diminishing budgets. Dr. Aslin thought for a moment.

"Have you tried prayer?"

We were talking about disciplining super-studs in the classroom, who later had to be sent to the principal's office, when an aspiring principal's questions kept escalating to the final one.

"What if it looks like nothing is working and the student finally tells you to go fly a kite?" Sensing the young man needed to mature in his thinking, Dr. Aslin responded, "Don't go."

In one of his summer classes, mid-lecture, the men suddenly rushed to the window and broke out into raucous laughter. I asked the fellow next to me what was going on.

"There's a streaker out there running through the water fountain. He doesn't have a thing on, and three policemen wearing gas masks and carrying clubs have him surrounded. (Stifling more laughter.) I wonder what they think he has concealed or what kind of gas they're going to get into anyway?"

It seemed the professors always had some kind of a friendly rivalry going on, mostly in relation to fishing and the secrecy of one's own hidden fishing hole. One time a professor refused to acknowledge that a second professor had caught the biggest fish of all and continued to ignore him. Undaunted, the second one carried his fish high over his head into the first one's Tuesday night class, turning it around so students could see it from every angle. Hardly looking up, the first one kept on lecturing, whereupon the second one walked over to him, plopped the dripping thing onto the middle of his desk, and walked out.

When one of Dr. Aslin's colleagues was promoted to chancellor, someone asked how he felt about his friend getting ahead of him in rank.

"Who, him? He's just great among equals."

I had another delightfully entertaining professor for several other classes as well, and was amazed and amused at some of his questions.

"If Columbia College closed down and you were going to help sell off the buildings, who would get the money?"

Or, "If you were to get a brain transplant, who would you be?"

Nothing was so revealing as to go out on one of his school surveys, where as a team, we gave feedback to the school on what we saw that was good and what we thought needed to be improved. The neighborhood school concept seemed to have the strongest foothold of all, and along with it, the reluctance to condemn, much less demolish, a school building no longer functional or safe. He would relate incidents where students were sitting on third floor unscreened window ledges with the windows open, or where an ancient school had an elm tree growing out the second floor, where a seed had lodged in some broken brick.

Doctoral exams would come soon enough, but in the meantime, I met the assistant principal from Neosho at a state principals' meeting at Tan-Tar-A. He told me his school was looking for a dean of girls just like the one who had been at Joplin. When I told him I was that very dean of girls, his eyes lit up like burning coals and we started talking.

By now I was teaching education courses almost full time, and wasn't wanting to leave my work undone toward helping the College gain four-year status in the education department. However, the call of a job I had once dearly loved, and a better salary to go with it, won out. We left for Neosho again during the first week of January, 1974.

Chapter 9

MY NOSE IN YOUR BUSINESS AGAIN

Neosho High School was about to greet its first high school woman administrator in charge of discipline, but it didn't know what title to give me that would satisfy the public. Director of student personnel services, dean of girls, assistant principal. Whatever worked, it was all the same job.

Jack Allman, just twenty miles away, was now the Joplin superintendent, and one of the assistant principals when I was dean of girls had also come back to the area. We were excited about having some of the clan back together, as Jack had already looked me up once during my last semester at Columbia College. He was on his way back from Jefferson City with one million dollars worth of bonds in the trunk of his car to take back to Joplin. I hadn't seen him for four and a half years and noticed how gray his hair had gotten. We were so eager to catch up on the news, I almost forgot to tell him we were going to move back to Neosho, so I had to run and peck on his car window as he started up his motor. He was really happy about that and wanted me to call him when we got there.

Before I got started on my job, I had a few things to learn, like not leaving extra programs in the gym after an assembly for students to make paper airplanes out of, but other than things like that, it was Parkwood High School all over again. The graffiti monsters were even more clever, as the bathroom walls were easier to write on.

Fire dragons smoked in the girls' restrooms, undaunted by female teachers forced to go in and check. The usual fights erupted from time to time, but they were fewer because the school was smaller.

The junior high was attached to the high school at the south end, giving ample opportunity for seventh and eighth grade girls to get into it with ninth graders. Most of it was over some boy, occasionally starting up on Friday night at the pool hall.

I mediated between two warring girls sitting on the other side of my desk. "Girls, I've been in this business for awhile, and there isn't much I haven't heard or seen. I have broad shoulders, plus I'm a pretty decent listener, so you can tell it to me any way you want."

There was an awkward silence, sniveling, and tears. "She called me a ratfink!" snarled the first one.

"She called me a scumbag!" said the other one, visibly shaking.

"He's *my* boyfriend and she's been hanging around to get him to look at her so she can take him away from me! He's mine!" claimed the first one.

I let the melodrama unfold for another five or ten minutes. Then I asked her, "How much did you pay for your boyfriend?" Heads jerked.

"Whaddya mean?"

"I'm sensing you feel some ownership here. How much did you have to pay someone to get him?"

"Nothin'. You don't hafta pay stuff to get boys."

"Then he's free to roam about the pool hall, no strings attached?"

"I guess." Some more talk from me about ownership. Finally she said, "Whattya gonna do about her calling me a ratfink?" I leaned back, looking very serious.

"Girls, this looks like the age-old Ratfink and Scumbag Controversy, and a few others like it, that have been going on for hundreds of years. Other nationalities have even gotten into it, until blood has run down the walls of apartment houses in at least one country. It just never seems to stop, and it looks like it's going to spread. What I'm confused about, though, is what you want from me. Would you like for me to decide which one of you is the ratfink and which one is the scumbag?"

Silence, weird looks, then giggles. "I'll bet you girls are smart enough to figure a way out of this all by yourselves, without any interference from me."

I confronted another almost-fight. This had gotten complicated just keeping the combatants sorted out. Jessica, a black girl, and a white girl named Cindy were into it over what had happened at a party. Cindy had snatched off Jessica's wig and publicly embarrassed her. To avoid a fight at the party, Jessica's mother, Molly, told Jessica that if she didn't beat up Cindy at school, that she, Molly, would beat the life out of her at home.

That posed a problem for me, since by the time they got back to school, neither girl really wanted to fight. I knew Molly and realized she could smash in a whole automobile if she wanted to.

Cindy was free to go so Jessica and I could figure this out. Jessica and I knew that if Molly found out Cindy hadn't been beaten up and Jessica punished, there would be worse than blood at home. Finally I told Jessica that if she were willing, I could quietly go to her teachers, not explain anything, and get her homework to take to in-school suspension for a day or two as a cover-up. Then I could send a report home to Molly, but never put a copy in the school files. Jessica cried tears of gratitude and relief.

Writing on the bathroom walls had now risen to Susan loves Mary instead of Susan loves Harry or Pete or Tom. I found some tracing paper, and after school, carefully copied as much graffiti as I could reach. I took pictures of what I couldn't. Then I made copies and sent them around to the English teachers for identification.

When restroom smoking reached a peak, I decided to have a little fun and take full responsibility for it. I asked my science major office girl if there would be any toxic or poisonous fumes resulting from dry ice hitting water. When the answer was no, I suggested it might be interesting if some little pieces of dry ice should happen to disappear from the science lab, and each find its way into a toilet in the center bathroom about thirty seconds before the bell rang.

That being accomplished, I meandered into the bathroom a minute after the bell. I could hardly keep a straight face, when I saw nine or ten freshman girls plastered against the wall, staring at smoke from the toilets rising to the level of their behinds. I scowled and said, "Well! I've told you girls over and over to quit smoking in here and now look what's happened!" They looked at me, clueless. I wandered out, hoping for something I could hide behind to conceal my stifled laughter.

I heard a voice from inside the restroom say, "You don't suppose that's dry ice, do you?"

One day the other assistant principal was gone, and I knew I had too much territory to protect. I headed for the farthest boys' bathroom and opened the door a bit to yell for anyone to come on out so I could lock it up. Twenty minutes later, a boy came to my office looking a little nervous. "Mrs. Hamilton, I think you've locked the band director in the boys' bathroom!"

When I had to supervise night ball games, our sons could come with me if they wanted to and watch while they did their homework. One night, at a girls' basketball game, three grade school boys were in the lobby right outside the gym door covering up giggles. I left my boys for a moment and checked. A large blacksnake had gotten out of the biology lab and was slithering around on the floor. The custodian was leaning on his broom, and I asked him if I could borrow it to catch the snake. "Ma'am, I've gotta have this broom right now to clean the floor at halftime so they can play on it again."

"Sir," I said, "please look at all those women up in the bleachers. If any one of them sees that snake, you're going to have a lot more than dust to clean up!"

I unlocked the biology door and got the cage, and a student helped me catch the snake. When everyone was gone, I sneaked down to the principal's office and left it on his desk without a note. Later I concluded that snake must have been retarded when I found him outside the school door with his mate's head down his throat, both successfully suffocating.

Not all problems involved discipline. One girl came to the office concerned about her mental state, confessing at one time she wanted to kill all of her baby kittens. This was a clue to ask her a question that proved to get to the heart of many of these matters.

"How much sleep have you been getting lately?" I asked.

"About four or five hours a night. Why?"

"What are you doing that is keeping you up so long?" Then she gave me a list of things that she felt she must do or else, much of it involving an excess of church work and work at home. This girl in my office, as with many students, didn't realize that certain chemicals in the brain needed for good mental functioning were depleted by the end of the day and could only be restored with the proper amount of sleep at night.

The next thing was to go over her list of things she thought she had to do and to try to eliminate some of them. The elimination of some church duties seemed impossible for her, but I posed the idea of postponing them for the time being and coming back to them after she graduated from high school and had more time. She managed to do that, and weeks later, a thank-you note slid under my door.

That year I fell in love with the biology lab's hooded rats. Years earlier, I had met one running loose in a friend's house and found out what an affectionate pet one could be. I was offered some adults to keep if I would return their babies when they got big enough. That netted the biology lab over a dozen baby rats, which I tried to smuggle back into the building inside a big grocery sack. Of course one of the counselors had to ask me what was inside the sack, and of course I had to show her.

A few female students had something to show too, as we were in the Age of the Braless Wonders. A dress code was still fairly enforceable in the middle seventies, and if something was showing that shouldn't be, the girl was sent home to make it right. One girl's ill-dressed mama took exception to this and met me in the school cafeteria to loudly proclaim her daughter's rights. Finally I said to her, "Ma'am, what would you think if I came to school without a bra?"

"But you're a respected member of the community." she objected.

"Thank you." I said. "Now, would you want any less than that for your daughter?"

I don't remember the nature of the confrontation with another girl, whose mother stormed past the principal's office and directly into mine. Her eyes rolling, and her bad breath even with my necklace, she started off with enough blasphemes to knock the feathers off a turkey. Unable to verbally undress me, she left to go down the hall to rough up one of the girl's teachers. I got the police on the phone, who got there barely in time to salvage the teacher's head of hair.

I had encounters two other times with girls' mothers. The first was after I also became yearbook sponsor. The school camera was broken, and I was taking snapshots with mine. A ruckus broke out in the bathroom, and without thinking, I stepped in with the camera hanging from my neck. The phone didn't stop for an hour after I got home, with all the mothers' voices coming from the same special education classroom. "Whaddya think yer doin' takin' pictures of my girl goin' to the bathroom?" Same song, different verse. I was patient because I didn't blame them.

The next episode involved a student who was constantly disrupting her English class. On a hunch I asked her, "Honey, are you acting up in class because you're having trouble reading?" The tears started to roll. I asked her how she would feel if I could get her into a special education class until she could get caught up. She was more than willing, but her mother wasn't. It was the old stigma. We jumped over the obstacle anyway, and it wasn't long before a clever teacher introduced her to the phonetics she had missed in first grade. After that, her discipline problems disappeared and soon she was sent back to regular classes.

My biggest challenge came one day when the local police pulled up in front of the school, each car with four of our girls in it. They had all been skipping school and had been caught throwing rocks at police cars. I knew them all and had a file card on each one. I realized something bigger had to happen than adding more punishment notes to their file cards. "Lord, I could use some help on this one," I said.

They sat around the big table in my outer office. "Girls, we have a lot of work to do, and no one can leave until we're finished here." I pulled out all my resources from my one counseling class and started my attack on esteem issues. I asked each girl, one by one, to turn to the girl on her right and to say something nice about her. By the time it was the third girl's turn, she started to cry. It had been so long! Among tears and laughter, serious, kind words went around in the other direction too, before they were done.

Then I had them divide a sheet of paper into four columns and put each of their four selves at the top. The self I think I am. Am I fooling myself here, maybe? The self others think I am. The old self-fulfilling prophesy that so many teenagers live by. The self I want to be. Those were their goals. The self I really am. The real me. They had to write things under each of the selves to see if the selves seemed similar or if one really stood out against the grain. As one would have guessed, they were living the selves others thought they were, and so much of it was negative. They had no clue to their own identities.

Eight more sheets of paper were handed out. Draw a line down the middle. Write negative on the left side and positive on the right. Now, you can't write anything on the left side. "But that's the side we know best," they cried. I know. Now write down ten positive things about yourself on the right. They were dumbfounded. They couldn't even start. I went around the circle, smiling, looking each girl in the eye, and saying something positive about her. Tears and smiles. It still took a long time for some to come up with even three.

I gave them until the next day to turn in a copy to me. "What will you do with them?" they asked. I would carefully study them and then put them in my bottom right drawer. If I even saw a gleam of wickedness in the eye of one of them, I would hold up ten fingers in the crowd to remind her of all the good things I knew about her. Their discipline problems soon took a nosedive down to twenty-five percent of what they were before.

In spite of a reduction in discipline problems, I was always on the alert at graduation time. Throwing up their hats at the end of graduation assembly didn't bother us nearly as much as spray cans of mystery stuff, obscene balloons, noisemakers, concealed rodents, and other such distracting mischief. It didn't take me long to learn that when they marched by to their chairs, if one hand was showing and the other one was drawn up into the sleeve of the graduation robe, there was almost always something concealed in it. They couldn't get past us without coughing it up.

Sometime earlier, we had learned to keep a closer eye on assemblies, when out of nowhere, a streaker came running across the gym floor with not much on except his tennis shoes and maybe three strings for a loincloth. However, the principal was on his toes and chased after him, catching him in his car just as he was ready to turn the key in the ignition. He grabbed the boy's hand, yanked out the keys, and apprehended him. Later the boys proudly gave the principal the name of Old Sneaky Shoes.

I had learned early on that students would find a nickname for you whether you liked it or not. I accidentally created my own one day when I was attending a teachers' meeting in Springfield. The teacher who was supposed to introduce an esteemed newswoman, who was to be one of the speakers, had to leave on an emergency and asked me if I would take over. I was decently dressed in a fancy pants suit, but felt a bit out of place, as the lady I was to introduce was wearing a long dress. So I hastily explained to the audience that I would have dressed more like her if it were not for the fact that one of my more enterprising colleagues told me I looked better in pants suits because they covered up my bird legs. By the next day, the nickname "Birdlegs" was all over school. I thought it was just as funny as they did, which didn't please them a lot.

Returning to Neosho put me back at the First Christian Church again. Our assistant pastor was a rather large, humorous, and very attractive woman named Martha Washington, a direct descendent of George Washington's brother. She had finally gotten wise to how to stop all the crank phone calls asking her about George and had listed her name in the phone book using her initials instead of the name Martha. Now she was in the midst of moving from one rental place to another, so that pranksters would quit coming to the door for the same reason. Several of us came over to help her clean up the house before she moved in. I was humming while I was scrubbing out the toilet, when I heard her laughing at me.

"What's so funny?" I asked.

"I've never heard anyone humming the Doxology before, while her head was in the toilet bowl."

A few months later, Martha and her mother had to make a hasty trip to Texas to attend a church meeting. Short of time, they quickly washed their only girdles and hung them outside overnight to dry. Someone stole them during the night.

"*Well!*" Martha growled. "Whoever stole them.........I hope they *fit!*"

Desperately needing a girdle, she called Sears from her hotel, explained her dilemma, and asked the male clerk if there were any way possible she could charge a certain brand and size girdle and have it delivered to the hotel.

"Sure," he said. "No problem."

It never came. After awhile, she quit fuming and started talking to herself. Martha, now put yourself in that clerk's shoes. If you were a male clerk, and someone named Martha Washington from another state called you from a hotel asking for an extra large girdle to be delivered to that hotel and charged, would you do it?

With that I began to pump more stories out of some of her ministerial colleagues. One from Marshfield told about a very old gentleman who had recently made his confession of faith and wanted to be baptized before he died. However, his eyesight was poor, and he feared he would not find his way out of the baptistery without his glasses, while the minister was rushing out to change his clothes to finish off the Palm Sunday service. So the minister rehearsed it all with him ahead of time, showing him how he could put his glasses up on the ledge and follow the ledge with his hand until he found them.

The choir director was up front leading the singing and stalling for time until the minister could get there. Then he heard a loud congregational gasp. The old man had not found his glasses and had crawled up on the ledge to locate them. With nothing on underneath his hospital gown attire, he knelt there, mooning the congregation! The poor flustered choir director ran over and grabbed a huge potted palm and dragged it in front of the old gentleman to cover him up.

Our choir was in the habit of processing in with the first hymn, and members did the best they could not to run into each other. A nearby choir stopped nothing short of perfection with its processional and had its march finely tuned. Halfway down the aisle, the long slender heel of one of the women caught in the furnace grating. Trying not to break the cadence, she slipped out of it and kept going. The chivalrous gentleman behind her bent over to snatch it up, and when he did, the whole furnace grating came with it, and he fell in.

I taught Sunday School for awhile for a mixed group ranging in age from seventeen to over seventy. In it were Newton Ford, an early-retired oil executive, and his wife, Anna Belle, who had recently moved to Neosho. Newton had Parkinson's disease like my father, but unlike Father, was doing everything the doctor ordered to keep in shape.

Going over to their house was interesting, not only because of all the crafts he was involved with, but because their house had a phantom toilet that flushed all by itself, usually during grace before lunch, or when someone was on the phone.

As Newton's Parkinson's progressed, he felt he needed some more entertainment. So he bought an extra-powerful set of binoculars and positioned himself at the breakfast table so he could lean his elbows on it and spy on our common neighbors between the slats in the Venetian blinds. But after awhile, I saw he wasn't using them anymore.

"Nope," he said. "The shaking got so bad I had to quit, 'cause it was making me dizzy."

PART II

Chapter 10

HE SHOULD HAVE GOTTEN A TROPHY

Jack Hamilton and I were divorced in the summer of 1976 after sixteen and a half years of marriage. It was the saddest moment in my life to be the one to break up the family. It had taken me two years to realize the fault was mostly mine, due to my erroneous thinking about marriage and thinking I could learn to fall in love. In the late fifties when I was of marriageable age, a girl was considered an old maid and not good enough to be picked out by a man if she was not married by her mid-twenties. I even asked my friends, what if you haven't found the man of your dreams by then? Their answer was to marry the best one you could. So I did to avoid the stigma.

I knew it was a mistake, but I pledged to keep my vows and stay with it. The relationship didn't do too badly for a number of years. He was a loyal father, but our own relationship had slowly deteriorated to the point of no return. Part of it related to his serious case of fading scruples, which made me think that I didn't want to spend the rest of a marriage watching him through bars. In the long run, he was extremely sad but gracious, and we stayed friends as we went our separate ways. Much later, his lack of scruples made me think of a TV host going around asking people if they had any. I wished I had remembered all of their responses.

"Yes, but I left them in my other purse."

"No! I've *never* had anything like that in my life!"

"I did once, but I forgot where I left them."

"Sure. I have them stacked all over my room. Whaddya asking me for? Go get your own."

"I might have had some when I was a kid."

"Yes, but I took some of my husband's medicine and got rid of them."

By the time we were divorced, Scott was thirteen, David eleven, and Dennis nine, all soon to have birthdays in the fall. They worked together as a team, all determined to protect their mother and make sure she wasn't forgotten on special occasions. They knew that the homes of school administrators were often targets for pranksters on Halloween, so Scott took the reigns as the oldest, put the lawn chair at the driveway entrance, dragged out the garden hose, and sat there ready to blast the enemy.

Without my realizing it, on my birthday, they sneaked out of the house while I was busy and walked to the grocery store to buy a cake and decorations with their pooled allowances. They got back just in time to quickly decorate the kitchen and light the candles before I knew what was going on. It was the most wonderful birthday I ever had.

The divorce was listed in the newspaper, so it was no secret. I wasn't looking for another husband, but who should come calling anyway, but an estranged cemetery lot salesman. Yeah, right. All I needed was a still-married man trying to lure me with a professed wad of money in the bank and a promise of his yet-to-happen divorce. I wondered if I were going to have to gnaw the telephone cord in half to get rid of him.

As time began to pass, the economy was beginning to deteriorate, and I was beginning to fear for my job. On the sly, I started looking for other opportunities, ranging from those of high school principal, assistant principal, placement director, and even director of a Latin American institution. Sometimes I was disappointedly interviewed only as the token woman, and other times, sought out by administrators with unholy intentions. Nothing seemed right.

Justifiably I began to panic. The economy finally did take my job, and I was left with a house to sell and no income beginning the following September. I prayed harder than I had ever done before and even went to the unemployment office, which I saw got to Scott emotionally. Then in August, the house suddenly sold. With a few thousand dollars in the bank, as a last ditch effort, I decided to move the boys and me back to Columbia to take classes toward certification in counseling. I found an apartment, and the Columbia school system let me place the boys in the school district where my parents lived so we could coordinate picking them up after school. Then Mother started slipping me some money from her Social Security check, claiming they were doing fine with their finances.

Now I was in a totally different situation. When I was studying to become an administrator, my colleagues kept telling me what a wonderful counselor I would make. Now my counseling classmates were telling me what an excellent administrator I would make. Was there ever going to be a real place for me?

Soon the money was going to be gone, and I wouldn't have enough for another semester without finding a job. However, another story had been unfolding. Jack Allman and I, always the dearest of friends and supporters of one another, had parted on a sad note when I left for Columbia. I didn't want to go, and he didn't want me to leave. He had just gone through a painful divorce two months earlier, and my leaving was about to cause him to lose one of his best friends. Not too long afterwards, he started buying plane tickets to Columbia to come see me and staying with my parents at night over the weekend. It was really too soon after his divorce for him to be totally comfortable with it, but somehow it was the right thing for both of us.

Then in December of 1977, over ten years after I met him, Jack Allman and I were married. We had been good colleagues together on the same path from the very beginning, always seeing eye-to-eye on school issues, child-rearing, money matters, fair play, and other basic values. He had helped me grow as an administrator, and after I returned to Neosho in 1974, I had spent long hours helping him on his doctoral dissertation, as he sought to complete the same degree I was working on. By the time he was divorced, his three sons, John, Jim, and Jeff were in or headed for college. I was thirty-nine and he was fifty, facing my children who were fifteen, thirteen and eleven. Someone should have handed him a trophy on our wedding day.

We pretended we didn't see what the Hamilton boys were doing to the car after the wedding. After all, I had taught them well about our family tradition to tamper with the bride and groom's car and suitcases. Mother the Sneak had started that trend at my first wedding, and knowing my past history, claimed I had it coming this time too. Among other things, she had poured toothpaste into my soap container, painted X's with clear nail polish on my glasses, and tied all my underwear in knots.

We moved into a rental house in Joplin, half-blinded by its red living room. When Jack first saw it, he thought it suggested a house of ill repute. He was anxious to finish out his ninth year as Joplin superintendent of schools, as things in the district were getting a little testy. He wanted to try at least one job overseas, if he could find one, before he called it quits.

Even with six kids, we briefly thought about having one of our own, but our ages and medications suggested otherwise. Finally he said, "I don't know if I want to be the only eighty-year-old at the PTA and on a cane." We both could live with that and concentrated on letting upcoming grandchildren satisfy the baby fix.

Jack and I had some catching up to do concerning stories about the growing up of each other's children and spent some time trying to make up for lost time. Scott was less than four years old when Dennis was born, and it hadn't dawned on him his mother was going to have a baby. When I told him where the baby was, he asked, "Did you eat the baby?"

Scott was the strategy player, the master of the chess game, and the scholar who tried to do everything right, including saving some of his allowance. David, his younger brother by twenty-one months, seemed serious on the outside, but underneath was the one most likely to play some silly prank on his younger brother. Having to do pushups in junior high for talking came as no surprise. This Mr. Neat wanted every hair in place, until serious curls started and it became unruly. Years later when he let it and his beard all grow out, I didn't recognize him and mistook him for the stove repair man. As David approached high school, he thought about becoming a mountain man and living in the woods in a log cabin when he grew up. At least he survived his childhood after eating Drano when he was four.

When Jack first met Dennis, he was walking to his bedroom with a hooded rat on his head with the tail hanging down between his eyes. Jack yelled, "Wash your hands! Wash your hair! Burn your clothes!"

Mr. Petting Zoo himself once sported a favorite Mickey Mouse hat, which fell into a national park outhouse when he looked down into it to see where his business had gone. He fully expected his father to get a ladder and go in after it and he sizzled underneath for the next two years when it didn't happen.

The winner of multitudinous hand-me-downs, Dennis was so grateful for a new pair of galoshes that he wore them to bed for a couple of nights. His new stepbrothers weren't nearly as grateful to have him around the first night five of the six boys met for a poker game, and eleven year old Dennis won most of their money. Jack made him give most of it back.

Jack's oldest and most serious, John, almost ended his life as a grade-schooler when the family moved to a farm in Sarcoxie. Jack had borrowed a boar that hadn't gotten the message yet that he was being borrowed to horse around with four new sows so they could populate the earth. If he had, the boar wouldn't have jumped out over the front of the truck to head south across I-44. When they finally caught him, John decided he was going to climb over the fence and ride him. Scared to death, Jack quietly said, "Wait Johnny, and I'll come over there and ride him with you." Jack walked over and lifted him up over the fence just in time.

Jim was Mr. Personality, who never caused a moment's trouble in school. However, a board member's son had broken his arm and had taken up spitting on any male classmates who said anything about it. If that brought a response from anyone, he'd hit him with his cast. Of course Jim eventually got spat upon, and went home to ask his father what to do about it. Jack figured Jim didn't have to put up with that, and told him to hit the kid in the nose the next time he did it. Jim's mother, Polly, looked unkindly on that suggestion, but it happened anyway, and both boys got suspended; Jim for only one day. The principal knew the situation and figured a lot fewer boys would have to be washing their clothes now that Mr. Spit had gotten the message.

Jeff was the jock, who, like most youngest children, had a room piled so high that mice could have three generations in there before anyone would ever discover them. Jack felt lucky if he could get the door open to see if Jeff were alive. One dark night, he ventured in and slipped on something slimy. Fearing the worst about what the dog had done, he turned on the light, only to find out it was half a peanut butter sandwich.

His father's school business wasn't of prime interest to Jeff, until the day Jack came home and was lamenting over the fact that unless things changed drastically, as many as twelve teachers in one elementary building might be fired. Somehow that got to Show and Tell, and after that, Bell Telephone must have made a fortune.

I never knew Polly, until we met years before at a Woman's Club meeting in Joplin. She and Jack had dated in high school and finally married when they were twenty. Like most couples after World War II, their money was scarce and they needed a vehicle.

Jack had a couple of friends who had an old Frito truck that they used for transportation around town. It had two bucket seats that weren't nailed to the floor too well, nor did they have any cushions. It was no prettier on the outside, as most of the exterior paint was gone. He finally bought it from them for something less than a couple of hundred dollars, thinking he could fix it up. After he scraped most of the rust off, he bought a gallon of black house paint because it was cheap, and gave it a good coat. The Frito logo burned through the paint, but that didn't keep him from driving it to church.

One Sunday, Polly, the ultimate lady, had gotten all fixed up to go to church, with long white gloves and the works. The clutch didn't work too well, and when Jack put on the gas, it lurched so badly it threw her backwards into the truck's old dirty back end. When she came up for air, she looked like she'd been in a bar room fight, which didn't make the Sabbath look so holy after all. After fifteen apologies from Jack, the clutch and the truck in general got more than their fair share of verbal abuse, and Polly's ordinarily lady-like demeanor turned into body language that could have filled a whole room for the rest of the day.

Another marriage happened about the time of Jack's and mine, that of my worldly female dog-factory named Spot, and Jack's nine-year-old celibate Labrador retriever named Duke. Duke's intentions were totally dishonorable, but Spot was already wise to a retarded suitor half her size who had a crooked tail, and who had sired other crooked-tails. Not to mention an assortment of strays resembling half-wolves, greyhounds and beagles. About the only thing that hadn't tried to mate with her was a porcupine.

Jack found he too had some things to get used to, or else ask for a change. Dragging our forks across our teeth when we ate made him cringe. So did my treatment of our quart-size tube of toothpaste we shared. He thought it should be squeezed from the bottom, instead of elbowed in the middle like I was doing.

We laid that to rest and got involved with Weight Watchers. The dogs didn't like the looks of that, because there went all the good scraps. I misunderstood the merits of Weight Watcher sugar substitute and must have used twice as much in the dessert. The dogs wouldn't even eat it.

Mother was totally fascinated with Jack. Stories from his childhood warmed and amused her first grade teacher heart, to the tune that she swore I should follow him around with a tape recorder. What stories he didn't tell on himself, his classmates made sure I knew about, as there seemed to be more horseplay than studying going on at Anderson High School during the war years.

As a child, Jack had good values, but was not prone to fully exercising them at school. Skipping school was a tempting option, even in late fall, and the lure of a swimming hole down at the river finally overtook him and eight of his buddies. When they got there, they took off all their clothes, hung them on the bushes, and gingerly stepped into the icy water. Their twig-infested clothes made a perfect cover for the superintendent who wasn't far behind.

"Since you guys have gone to all this trouble, I suggest you stay in for at least another thirty minutes to make it worth your while. I'll wait, and when you're all done, I'll expect you back in my office."

As to Jack's participation in sports, his classmate Jack Cunningham said Jack was the only basketball player who could trip over a painted line. Max Mitchell, a second one, named him "Ox" after he threw a discus through a science window and later fell down with all his gear going aboard ship in the Navy.

His coordination improved, which was a good thing, as he eventually misguided himself into dental school. He didn't know what else to do for a living, except to do what his brother was already doing, which looked like it would at least be lucrative. He loved the biological sciences, but had second thoughts about having to deal with cadavers. That didn't seem to bother his lab partners. By the time they got to the last stages of cutting theirs up, Jack never knew what the next day would bring. After he found his wearing a Derby hat one morning, he started paying more attention.

He was telling his friend, Earl the sheriff, about this one morning over coffee, when Earl confessed to a fast one he'd played on their friend, Fred, the game warden. Fred's aversion to dead bodies was about the same as Jack's, but Earl told Fred he really needed him to help carry a body downstairs that had been discovered the night before. Fred balked, but Earl told him the guy didn't weigh much, and they could get the job done in no time. What he didn't tell Fred was that the body had been there nearly a month and had about melted into the mattress, causing Fred to almost blow a gasket when he got up there.

Many years earlier, when Jack's father was the mayor, as well as owning one of the local grocery stores, the town almost lost their colorful citizen, Harry, who couldn't seem to keep out of jail. Finally Harry got pretty tired of being incarcerated and of life in general, and said to Jack, "Go tell your daddy I'm going to hang myself." Frightened, Jack ran at top speed to the grocery store to tell his father, who was too busy to listen, even after a second attempt to get his attention. Fearing the worst, Jack hurried back to the jail to check on Harry, who said, "Little Allman, what did your daddy say?"

"He didn't say anything."

"Tell him I really mean it!" said Harry.

Jack finally got Charlie's attention. However, Charlie was still busy, plus wasn't too impressed with threats like Harry's, and said, "Tell him to go ahead." Jack ran back, and sure enough, Harry was hanging by his belt, gagging, and with his tongue hanging out. When he finally got his father to come down to the jail, Charlie said, "Well, go tell the Marshall to cut him down. He's gonna live."

About five years later, after returning from the Navy, Jack was in the local barbershop getting his hair cut and telling this story, without mentioning Harry's name. Some customer finally asked him who the guy was, and before Jack could get the fellow's name out, he suddenly realized it was Harry who was cutting his hair.

"I don't remember," he said, as he felt the monster razor gliding up and down the back of his neck.

Charlie's brother-in-law, Fritz, was his partner in the grocery store business, and the two weren't adverse to hiding a bottle of whiskey for themselves in a storage room in back of the store. They didn't nip at it too often, but soon the whiskey level started going down faster than the nips would suggest. Fritz thought Charlie was doing it, but since he wasn't, Charlie suspected a nice old wino they knew. So when the whiskey level got down considerably, Charlie put something foul-tasting in the bottle to raise the level a bit and waited. The next day, the wino came roaring in from the rear of the store, screaming and cursing and threatening to do bodily harm. Not wanting to fight him, Charlie and Fritz ran out of the store, up Main Street, and into the pool hall, getting momentarily stuck together in the door. The wino was having a hard time running because his toes had been frozen off one time when he was drunk, but he gained an edge when he grabbed up some billiard balls and threw them at the two as they were running out the back door.

Some of Charlie's other relatives weren't so lucky with their escapes. I became a little concerned, when I found out how many had died from unnatural causes. An older brother, riding near Springfield in the back of a truck, made a lunge for his hat after the wind blew it off, and fell off the truck and died. Another scene involved a saw mill, where the relatives had hooked up the timber saw to the motor of an old truck to get it to work. One day it came loose and flew into the forehead of a teenage nephew, killing him. A third relative, a salesman, was running across the yard and failed to see a clothesline before it caught him in the throat. He died fewer than twenty-four hours later.

Jack's great-uncle had already lost his wife and was making some morose statements about which book his funeral money was hidden in. He was very sick and was paying close attention to his pearl-handled gun. One morning, the milk and egg boy knocked on Jack's parents' front door, claiming he had peeked into the great-uncle's window when he didn't answer the door, only to find that things didn't look right. The man had indeed shot himself dead, but five shells on the floor suggested misfires. Jack's mother offered Jack and a friend twenty dollars to get rid of the stained couch and clean up the rest of the mess.

Years later, when we were sorting family treasures and getting ready to move again, Jeff saw the gun on our kitchen table and decided to add a little drama.

"I can just see it now. The guy points the gun to his head, pulls the trigger, and says 'Oh drat!' Then he points again, misses, and says 'Bummer!' Then he points a third time and it goes off into the air. Then a fourth and ...."

Unfortunately, Anderson didn't have a regular embalmer in those days, and funeral embalming was done by the local plumber. It was common to have a twenty-four hour watch at home, with everyone sitting around for hours, taking shifts. You'd think the corpse was going to escape out the front door.

When Jack's grandfather died, the plumber was called while the relatives were gathering. They figured when he was finished, he would leave by the back door. But later he and his two buckets of blood and accompanying paraphernalia came traipsing through the living room amid a group of gasping women as he headed out the front.

Jack's relationship with his father, Charlie, had been pretty strained while he was still living at home. Charlie was of the old school, where you didn't waste time burning any daylight, got up with the chickens, came home at noon, wolfed down lunch, then went back at it until dark.

Charlie said little and didn't spend a lot of time paying attention to what his own family did. In fact, when Jack asked him who some of his relatives were that might live nearby, Charlie responded, "I don't know, because if they're not hungry or in jail, they don't need me." Even later, after Jack and Polly had children, Charlie would take it just so long and finally give each of the grandchildren a nickel to get lost. As much as he secretly loved them, his borrowed philosophy was that fish and relatives begin to stink after three days. When Charlie finally figured out that Jack wasn't destined for the penitentiary, they finally started having a pretty good relationship until Charlie's death.

Not too long after Jack's mother, Helen, passed away after a long battle with heart failure, Charlie married Oleta. Her husband had passed away down in Arkansas, and one of her friends had asked her what kind of a man she might be looking for. She said, "A Baptist, a Democrat, and a Mason, but not necessarily in that order." Her friend's nose pointed to Charlie, who was of similar leanings in hunting for a wife. It had also been suggested by Helen before she died, that he align himself with someone who would make him change his underwear and his socks when he was supposed to.

Knowing how he felt about relatives, it came as a family surprise that Charlie would spend so much time helping Ruby, Oleta's sister, who came with the package. He bought a little furnished house for her to live in and kept her stocked with firewood and cigarettes. Ruby had a heart of gold; however, had a voice that would make a hippopotamus jump. By the time I entered the scene, she and Oleta were just old enough to start having squabbles. One started while Jack and I and the neighbor across the street were all having lunch with Oleta and Ruby after church. Ruby started it by claiming she'd had to pay Oleta thirty-five dollars a month rent on her house.

"You did not. You only paid me twenty-five dollars!" Oleta retorted.

"Did not!"

"Did too! I lowered it after your husband died in June."

"My husband didn't die in *June!* He died on.......Memorial Day,...... September 3!

The neighbor looked at us with one eye. "I've even tried prayer, and it doesn't work," she said. After everyone left, I stayed with Oleta for awhile to help with some things around the house.

She said, "How about you staying for supper, and let's just eat scraps." About an hour after that, she was rummaging around in the refrigerator and said, "Hey we forgot something for our supper."

"What?"

"There's still some cat food in here."

A few days later, I picked up Ruby to take her to our house for awhile for a visit. When I pulled up into the drive, a dead rodent was lying in the driveway. Ruby wouldn't get out.

"He's dead, Ruby."

"No matter. You can take me home."

Jack was a little relieved. He'd already had enough of her after she got onto him at Oleta's house for not washing off all the dinner dishes before he put them in to soak.

Jack's brother, Doc, lived nearby, but was obviously missing out on some of the fun. Doc's birthday was approaching, yet we were all just old enough not to need much of anything, so we were having a hard time figuring out what to give him. Since he and Margaret traveled some, we settled on a pair of his and her travel urinals, which we wrapped up in a shoe box.

We drove down to Noel where his dental office was and caught him in the alley behind it, smoking a cigarette after he'd sworn he was going to give up smoking. That caught him off guard, and when he sat in the back seat of our car to open up his gift, he mumbled, "You know, if I were in a good mood, I might think this was funny."

He got even with Jack the next Christmas by giving him a Bombay taxi horn that would raise Lazarus, and a box with Dave's Fish Caller in it. Jeff thought that was all too amusing and grabbed it and started calling fish out from under the couch.

With his history, no one really knew what prompted Jack to eventually become a superintendent of schools and try to corral the kids that were doing some of the same things he did at their age. One of the more colorful scenarios was at Sarcoxie, Missouri, where Jack had just taken over as superintendent, and where things were reaching a chaotic peak. Someone came in to inform him that a student was down in the boys' restroom smoking and wouldn't come out.

Jack went down to take care of it and found him there, sitting on the toilet with his pants down around his legs.

"Come on, son, put out the cigarette. We're going to the office."

"Not until I've finished this cigarette, supe." he said.

Jack was pretty hot tempered in those days, and this obviously didn't sit well. He swung at the cigarette to knock it out of the kid's mouth, but accidentally caught the kid on the side of the head, unintentionally knocking him down onto the hot steam pipes running between the toilets. The boy yelped and tried to get up, but every time he did, his legs kept getting tangled up in his pants. When the boy's father came to get him later, he wasn't exactly pleased with the color of his son's rear, but figured he deserved it.

Students weren't the only thing Jack had to watch out for. He was playing cards one night at a buddy's house, when he got a phone call that the alarm on the school safe was going off. With the suggestion from his friends not to leave unarmed in the dark, he rushed out to his car. It started, but wouldn't go, no matter how hard he pumped on the gas pedal. Unknown to Jack, the whole thing was a setup, as one of the board members, who owned a nearby car dealership, had gotten his mechanic to bring over a long-handled car jack so he and his buddies could hoist up the car's rear end off the ground a couple of inches while Jack wasn't looking.

After we were married, Jack expressed his secret desire to try for an overseas job before looking for any other opportunities in the States, so he started applying while we were still in Joplin. He was finally offered the chance to compete for the superintendency at the American School in Teheran, Iran. His first prerequisite was a cholera shot that sent him into orbit and begged the sympathies of one of his administrative colleagues, who came over to console him, since he'd been through that before.

When Jack could stand up again, he got on the plane and found himself in a country where a lot of the running water ran through open flumes resembling huge gutters. People might be drinking from them, washing clothes, or skinning an animal. Public toilets were extremely clean, but something you wouldn't want your mother or wife to have to maneuver, as there was only a hole in the floor and a shower hose for cleaning.

The superintendent's home was a palace with china, crystal, silverware, furniture, servants, an aviary, and a marble driveway. The salary in 1978 was $100,000 a year plus a lot of perks. However, there were drawbacks concerning the school and the city. A new school building was being cemented together with a common mix of camel dung and straw. Students were necking and worse in the school yard. Downtown posted monthly signs as to how many people had been killed in traffic. If there weren't enough traffic lanes, drivers made extras. If you wanted to cross a street, you were safer if you did it in lock-step with a nun. Jack wanted the job anyway.

Competition was stiff among the four candidates, and eventually Jack ran second, with Bill Keough from Boston getting the job. Jack flew home and handed me the "loser's prize" he'd bought; a small brass statue of a bearded Iranian wearing a turban and riding his jackass backwards, using his tail for reins. Years later, an Iranian gentlemen saw it in my office and started laughing when he heard the story. "Those people are in power now!" he cried.

Bill Keough eventually became one of the Iranian hostages. The school in Iran had closed down, and he had moved to another one. The American Embassy in Teheran called him one day to see if he could get off to come down and finalize some school records before they were shipped out of the country. The morning of his arrival, he was taken hostage along with the others.

Jack could have been Bill if he'd gotten the job.

One morning before school, I answered the phone and it was Jack Hamilton. He was in town with my sister, Janet. I didn't know he even knew where she lived. He said they were going to get married in March. There was silence, then strange noises in the house.

Finally Scott said, "What'll we call him? Uncle Dad?" Their father was about to become their mother's brother-in-law, and their aunt was going to be their stepmother, and my sister was going to be the wife of my ex-husband. It worked out better for us all just to get along and let it go at that. Then Jack and I wondered what the next moves would be. He was certain he didn't want my ex-husband as a relative, but he knew we couldn't exclude my sister either. Were we destined to see each other only at weddings, funerals and hangings? We had ground rules to start working on.

Soon afterwards, Jack resigned as Joplin superintendent, but none of the other overseas jobs he'd applied for had come through. He was disappointed when neither Greece nor Kenya called, but decided he could live without Kenya's tsetse fly and the hotel across the water nicknamed the Dysentery Arms. Finally someone called him from Iberia, Missouri, where he'd had his first superintendency, to see if he would be interested in coming back. Mother hadn't heard of Iberia and wondered if he meant Siberia. Jack thought about it for a long time and finally accepted.

Iberia had fond memories of Jack. He had chaperoned a group of unruly school boys on a trip, including an overnight. They took turns showering, and as Jack was toweling off, he failed to see a camera going off. A few days later, a citizen called him to meet with a group of men in front of the Post Office. He saw a large crowd gathered in front of a near life-size stark-naked poster of himself that had been nailed to a big tree not far away. Some of the men were posted as guards so it wouldn't be removed.

By the time our family arrived in Iberia in 1978, the crowd of men had dwindled to a few who met at noon in the local establishment to eat, spit tobacco juice in paper cups, and shoot the bull. An old buddy sometimes led the charge, but he was so hard of hearing, that he would yell, "I'm half deaf, darn it! If you want my attention, you're going to have to rattle a bush!"

Since I did the grocery shopping, I bought Jack's chewing tobacco. I didn't know Jack had been pulling the grocery boy's leg, until he asked me, "Mrs. Allman, is it true you chew a whole carton a month?"

Dennis, David, and Scott Hamilton

Chapter 11

MOVING TO ARGENTINA OR HONK IF YOU'RE A TERRORIST

Jack finally got his wish for an overseas job ten days after he took the Iberia position. The president of the Board of Education in Buenos Aires called on the ninety-eight degree day I was moving the rest of our belongings out of our Joplin apartment. The American School, also called Lincoln School or Asociación Escuelas Lincoln in Spanish, was associated with the Department of State in Washington and needed both a superintendent and a counselor, plus one of us needed to know Spanish.

He interviewed us both in Chicago, and we negotiated hard. Our whole family and all our belongings, including children and dogs, were to be transported to a waiting house at the school's expense. Due to inflation, we would only be paying a part of the monthly rent. We would be given a month's home leave each year. A school car would be available most of the time, although the house was only four blocks from school. We had only twenty-one days to get out of the country if we wanted it. Unknown to us, we were about to walk into the last throes of a military junta and fading terrorism.

We did, but it was some leap of faith to consent to going to a strange country, strange school, and promise of a home, and to take three teenagers with us, one who would have been happier dipped in turpentine. Our dogs were the size of mountain lions, and it was no small feat to get them caged and transported without giving them or their handlers a heat stroke.

As a Spanish major, my vision of Latin American public transportation had been limited to buses carrying sweaty bodies, goats, chickens, sombreros, lengths of rope, and small suitcases. On the contrary, when we got to the Lan Chile terminal in Miami, we were totally surprised to find an assortment of beautiful women clad in real fur coats. They were mixed in with the men and children, some of the latter wearing Mickey Mouse hats or carrying large sacks of souvenirs in addition to big suitcases. We had been alerted that the seasons in Argentina were just opposite those of the States and had worn sweaters. Now, lacking fur coats, I was beginning to wonder if we shouldn't have purchased fur-lined, battery-charged underwear.

South American tourists who have just been to Disneyland are wound up like Energizer batteries and don't stop just because it's dark. I had yet to learn that this wasn't just a phenomenon of Disneyland overdose, but a way of life, starting with supper anywhere from 6 to 9 p.m. and ending with supper still going anywhere from 9 p.m. to midnight. No wonder they had to take siestas to recover.

Sometime in the wee hours, I managed to drop off to sleep and chose to stay that way while Jack and the boys got off the plane to roam around the airport in Santiago, Chile. They came back bearing beautiful little China ornaments, but quivering as if they had been chased by rabid werewolves. When they had tried to get back on the plane, they didn't understand the Spanish orders belted out by the guards, and the next thing they knew, machine guns were in their ribs.

Disembarking at Ezeiza International Airport in Buenos Aires was certainly less threatening, with only the fear left of not being recognized by those who were supposed to pick us up. They really couldn't miss us, as Jack was taller than anyone there, except for a Swedish man who looked like he'd been having bad dreams. The second worry was getting through customs with ten giant suitcases and our carry-on luggage, enough by itself to have downed the plane.

Much to our surprise, the customs agent only went through two suitcases before he waved us on. We were much luckier than a woman we heard about later, who thought that the better mousetrap might not exist in Argentina, and had brought in a huge suitcase stuffed to the brim with tampons, lined up like cordwood. Unknown both to us and to her, terrorism had just about ended, but no one was taking any chances. The near whiskerless young customs agent had barely peeked into the suitcase, when he started to tremble. He asked her for her passport and then took another frightened peek. Quickly he shut the lid down again and asked her if she had anything to declare. Confused, she said no. Then he gingerly opened the lid again, slipped one of the tampons out, peeled off the paper, took out his cigarette lighter, and lit the string. He threw it to the far corner of the room, covering his head and ears, waiting for it to explode.

Since we had sent pictures in advance, our benefactors were there waiting for us, having already picked up the dogs, who were waiting for us in a truck at the house. I was fearful I would say something inappropriate with my Spanish that I hadn't used for seventeen years, but I had plenty of time to do that later. Luckily the bilingual elementary principal, who later became our chief informant when we said anything wrong, was also there to meet us. The Board president and his wife had been kind enough to loan us some minimal furniture until our shipment arrived, and my secretary, Graciela, whom I had yet to meet, had left warm empanadas in the oven for us to eat, which were absolutely wonderful.

After we had made the rounds and had been introduced to the school and to the faculty, the elementary principal asked me to please say a few words on behalf of Jack to the elementary faculty, who knew very little English. I gave it my best shot with my academic and very Mexican vocabulary, wondering why there was a polite smile or two. I stressed what a good man my husband was, how glad we were to be there, and how proud we were to be guests in their beautiful country. Later I learned that instead of telling them what a wonderful man my husband was, I had lauded his virility.

The next step was to figure out how and where to buy groceries. We lived in the suburb of La Lucila, which had a string of specialty food shops a few blocks from the house. To get there and to buy any quantity at all, we had to borrow the nine year old school car, which someone had named "Hesitation Red." Jack's secretary was already working up a list of dirty words to retort to the list used by Argentine motorists toward careful drivers. I already knew that in Cuba, the ultimate insult was to call someone a dog of a bad race; however, that would only be laughed at by Argentines. If you really wanted to get under someone's hide, you had to call him a vegetable, like a carrot or an old cabbage. I learned later, that could also get you killed.

One store contained only meat, vegetables, and fruit. The shopkeepers loved and trusted Americans, and were more than kind about helping us to get past the language barrier. When I asked for three of the pineapples hanging up overhead, they started laughing, pantomiming that I had just asked for three punches in the nose.

I didn't recognize some of the meat behind the counter and found out later that there wasn't much belonging to a cow that an Argentine wouldn't eat. A year or so later, when son Jim came to live with us, he asked me if I would go buy him some testicles. I told him the Spanish word for them and said, "*You* go ask the butcher for testicles!" Jim had already experienced intestines, when he and Jack tried to grill them at a Boy Scout outing, and the intestines had tried to crawl off the grill like snakes.

I did have a little fun at the butcher's expense, when I walked in one day wearing my fake fur coat. Not recognizing fake fur, he asked me what animal that had been. Trying not to laugh, I said, "Bear." He looked at me for a long time.

"What did you do with the meat?"

"I put it in the freezer."

"How big is your freezer?" asked by a man who knew nothing more than the usual tiny freezers associated with very small Argentine refrigerators.

"Big enough to put five bodies in," I said. He looked startled. Then I had to confess I was teasing him and that it wasn't bear, and also explain the concept of fake fur. I did reassure him we actually did have a freezer that big, since we had brought it from the States.

At first I had to go three suburbs away to buy fish. As I walked along, a small octopus smiled at me from behind a window, waving toward an assortment of indescribable monsters, one of which looked like he could have eaten a small car. The fact that they were all dead didn't diminish their accumulated ferocity. The people inside were all singing and waiting on people as fast as they could run. From twelve feet away, a decapitated corvina sailed through the air and onto the counter, where it was to be wrapped and paid for. A man scaling fish off in the corner was making jokes and singing love songs to a pile of tuna heads. Someone off to one side flopped a big one onto the scales, making a fur-clad lady jump.

"Sorry, that one was still alive!" he joked.

Later Graciela took me to her favorite food stores, which unlike ours, were not housing stray cats posing as food inspectors. Since we had such a big freezer, I could buy large quantities, and as I was doing so, I suddenly noticed the price was dropping. When I started to question the grocer's math, Graciela gave me a courteous nudge, politely telling me in English to keep quiet, as the grocer thought I had a restaurant and was giving me the restaurant discount.

The same worked in another fish store, where I used my same line about the freezer. I asked for *diez kilos* of fish (22 pounds), as I was boycotting a price hike on beef. The butcher kept trying to rid me of my faulty Spanish and convince me I should be asking for *tres kilos* (about six and a half pounds). Spooked about the size of our freezer, he couldn't load my fish into the car fast enough and get rid of me.

Cooking all this was no small feat, as our new stove had arrived damaged beyond repair, and the small gas stove that came with the house had no temperature controls on it except for low to high. The marks might have been in centigrade anyway, which certainly would have beaten having to crawl on the floor to judge the height of the gas flame every time. Raising and lowering the flame got to be a chore, and it worked better to leave the flame constant and to stick a match box in the oven door to let the heat out whenever I needed to lower the temperature.

Since we had so many groceries to haul home, often on foot, I bought a folding cart on wheels and later a couple of large baskets from a peddler who parked his horse-drawn cart on our grass so his horse could have lunch and fertilize the lawn. Food was much like it was in the States, only some of it was much bigger and better. The cows were all grass-fed, which added a marvelous flavor to beef. Fruit and vegetables appeared to be on steroids. Squash was so large it looked like it could be carved into lawn furniture. Bakery products looked like works of art, until you noticed the missing salt. The ordinary French-style bread was delicious the first day, but watch out after that, as it hardened into missile quality. We gave some to Duke to gnaw on, and it was so hard, he took it over to the swimming pool and soaked it.

At first there were no frozen foods, and when they finally arrived a year or two later, they had been shipped in from Canada. Cottage cheese first came into the country while we were there, and we were introduced to Argentine *dulce de leche* or milk jam. As I understood it, it was milk that had been boiled down to a caramel-like state. I didn't know what to do with it, but found people putting it on a little bit of everything.

There were essentially no salad dressings except for catsup, mustard, and a mix of the two. Consequently I made up a recipe I had brought from the States and gave some to Graciela. Later, when I asked her how she and Hector liked it, she said, "Hector deedn't poot eet on dee salad – he poot eet on dee meat."

Argentine men took great pride in their outdoor culinary arts. It was usually they who were in charge of the *asado*, or meat cooked outdoors in a grill area all to itself, often partially bricked-in and with a roof. Another American friend never did get it right whether the grill or the person grilling was called an *asador* or whether that referred to some aspect of his pedigree; nonetheless, there was a fierce and friendly competition among men as to who was the best one and who cooked the best *lomo*. Beef were butchered differently in Argentina, and when you asked for the prize cut called *lomo*, you got a long section composed of the most tender parts of all the other cuts. The grill was ready for it when you could hold your hand over the charcoal at the level of the meat, and after five seconds, your hand was too hot.

Next to the outdoor grill was the pool, which at first we thought was a middle-class luxury, until summer came, and what air conditioning we had, wheezed and gasped for lack of sufficient electricity. Then you could use the pool to cool off, or as in the case of the neighbors, to fall into after partying for three hours and eating too much *lomo*. The biggest challenge was having to use a transformer for anything electrical, as the whole house was wired for 220. While I was fiddling with the living room lamp, one of our sons quipped, “Mom, why don’t you put that plug in your ear and see if your nose lights up?”

The upstairs was interesting. The bathroom off our bedroom had a bidet, something I had never seen before. We had been assured by someone that it was not a water fountain. Before you got to the bedrooms, there was a balcony just like you saw in the old movies. Jack used it later to make family announcements in his underwear, a long beach towel around his head, Arabian style. There was a patio area off David’s room, with vines strong enough for a burglar to climb. A safe was embedded in our tiny bedroom closet, where we locked up our pesos for the month. Fortunately there was another little closet at the end of the balcony, where I could hang my clothes. Unfortunately our house was joined to the one next door via a thin wall, so that on occasions, it sounded like they were playing roller derby in there.

When the furniture finally arrived six weeks later, the load was missing everything that hadn’t gotten onto the manifest by the time we made our hasty exit from the States. Monopoly money was scattered everywhere to make it look like a robbery. Some furniture had gouges in it; however, it was later repaired by expert Argentine craftsmen.

Argentines seemed to have a love affair with anything that came from the States. The movers even wanted to stay and watch us unpack boxes so they could see what was in them. Since practically everyone had a maid, we were lucky enough to find a good one for a day and a half a week, and she wanted to work extra so she could help us unpack and see what was in the shipment. Even the neighbor children started to peek through the wrought iron fence, coveting the big empty boxes that were beginning to stack up. I made a deal with them. You teach our dogs Spanish and you can have all these boxes. We'll even cut holes in them for eyes for you. It was a deal. Lines of boxes crawled down Vicente Lopez Street, giggles pouring out of the holes.

I wasn't kidding about teaching the animals Spanish. No dog that I knew of around there knew English. I used that information later in pet stores in the States, when I couldn't get parrots to talk to me. If a parrot ignored me, but suddenly I became his valentine by speaking Spanish to him, it was highly likely he had been caught somewhere south of the border and not hand-raised in the States as claimed.

There seemed to be a thing about neighbors in our middle class neighborhood that suggested they should make every effort not to know each other. Almost every house was surrounded by privacy fences or hedges. If you wanted to socialize, you had to go to someone's house you already knew from church or work.

Some hedges offered only partial seasonal screening, as there was a variety of giant ants that used their leaves for some unknown ant project down the street. You would have to dodge columns of them marching down the sidewalk, moving leaves perched overhead like monster umbrellas. They weren't the only things into construction. Practically every block had one house with a dirt or sand pile in front of it, which didn't get any shorter, because the project was always going to be finished *manana manana* (tomorrow) or *manana* (later). *Manana* sometimes didn't come the next year either.

Depending on the season, we could watch the pink rose tree, or the huge hibiscus bloom, or see the lemons ripening. There were tropical plants, palm trees, calceolaria, cineraria, and nasturtiums in the yards. A gardener kept everything looking beautiful and finally even quit cutting himself with his shears whenever Duke looked at him.

Giant poinsettia bushes grew to two stories tall, blooming in June, when it was winter and the days were short. Everything else was backwards too, due to the opposite seasons, so that Christmas came when it was hot. Finding a real Christmas tree was next to impossible, leaving only some puny artificial ones for sale, barely harboring a few bristles per branch. People couldn't wait for Christmas dinner to be over so they could go outside and jump into their pools to cool off.

We were soon aware that every major celebration involving Jesus was marked by noises resembling firecrackers and bombs going off. It was hard to decipher what was a resurgence of terrorism and what was elation over Baby Jesus being born in the manger. The day some real bombs went off, I had to look at the calendar to make sure it wasn't something holy.

I was innocently cooking breakfast early one morning, when I thought I heard what sounded like bombs, machine guns, and more bombs. I ran upstairs to see if Jack had heard the same thing. He had, and the noise wasn't stopping. When we got to school, we found out that some leftover terrorists had targeted the Minister of Finance's house in Olivos, one suburb away, diminishing it to barely a three foot pile of rubble. The family, and even the dog, escaped serious injury. However, our money changer, who lived next door, came to the school with bullet holes in the side of his car. Sometime later someone said a house a couple of blocks from us had been targeted, but we never heard it.

We wouldn't have been surprised to have heard trouble in the air, as Peron's second wife was under house arrest in Olivos. From the commuter train going back and forth to the Capitol, we could see that some of the fences in that area weren't mere hedges, but stone walls fortified with barbed wire or rows of broken glass on top. In earlier times one had to be careful riding the train, as even hanging one's arm out the window might result in the quick loss of a wrist watch or piece of jewelry.

In quieter times, we could safely watch the local dynamics each time the train stopped at another suburb. On one trip, I spied a buxom lady, with a low-cut v-neck sweater on, walking along with a middle-sized parrot's head peeking out of it. We often took the commuter train instead of the car, especially when we needed to go to the Capitol. There was a nice, Chinese restaurant on the way, where the food was wonderful, but the communication to get any wasn't. The owners didn't know English and only a little bit of Spanish, so if we told them we wanted egg rolls, we got funny looks. I finally figured out, that if we asked for *empanadas*, they got the message. At some of the other downtown restaurants, we found out the sky was the limit when it came to what might appear in a salad, like beets, cold peas, and pineapple, or palm hearts and some nameless thing.

Of course a good American movie had to follow a meal, as long as we could be assured the sound would be turned up loud enough so the Americans could hear it. Sometimes the Spanish, dubbed in at the bottom was such a misfire translation, I would start laughing, causing Jack to think he'd missed a punch line. By the time I'd get done explaining, we'd be lost as to where the plot was going, and the audience would be wondering why I was the only one laughing in the first place.

I thought about our first downtown movie with the minister and his wife, who drove us through traffic resembling that of Los Angeles. We were grateful for the ride, as the school car at best was riding like a Brahma bull. The only seats left in the huge movie house were in the first two rows, which for all practical purposes, were under the screen. Our whole second row had to lie down in the seats and practically look straight up. Jack thought he put his foot in some lady's left ear in front of him because she got up and stomped off.

Our first visit to the Colon Theater to see *Romeo and Juliet* by Gounod was a whole lot better, as a student, Jade York, and her mother, Joyce, invited us up to their apartment ahead of time to hear Andy Griffith's version to get us mentally prepared. Jack wasn't prone to going to operas, but Joyce figured this would shed a whole new light. We had box seats so Jack could sit in the back and chew, still thinking he wasn't going to like the real version. He got so interested in the production and in watching for the pea vine Andy said Romeo had "clumb up," that he sat transfixed. He waited breathlessly for the death scene, dramatically wiping his eyes so all the other box holders could see him. He was really stifling tears of laughter, because Romeo didn't know that after he poisoned himself, he wasn't supposed to keep popping up off the floor and singing arias like he was the church soloist. Whether it was after the movie or after the opera, if we decided to stay up for Argentine coffee, we might as well get ready for the caffeine jitters and a long sleepless night.

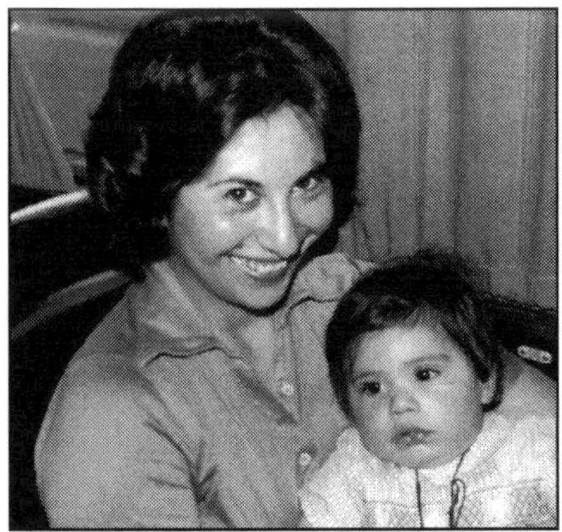

Graciela and Juan Pablo

School emblem

Chapter 12
DROPPING THE BALL

The process of becoming legal seemed beyond description and certainly not according to Hoyle. On Monday, we made a one hour trip to the Buenos Aires capitol to get driver's licenses, only to be told to come back Tuesday. This was supposed to beat standing in line for two or three days waiting for them to get processed in the suburbs, while we grilled our meals on the sidewalk. In the meantime, for reasons unknown to us, we'd been instructed to tell anyone stopping us that we lived at the Bank of America.

A "007" from the bank did a fine job of getting our visa paperwork through and keeping us out of jail. If we were stopped, we were supposed to dish out a number that said our visas would be stamped into our passports on Tuesday. Then we could do something with our licenses on Wednesday. Once legal, we'd no longer have to carry bogus letters in Spanish from the elementary principal, posing as the superintendent, stating we were visitors of the school and had permission to drive the school car.

Now that all the red tape was cut, Mr. 007 said, "Let the fingers do the work for you," meaning those finishing up the paperwork. Jack started calling him "Fingers." At Immigration, we went upstairs for a medical checkup. We had to answer to: Are you dead or alive? Name? Nationality? Wear glasses? What for? Operations? All other categories were bypassed, and a weird little man signed it with a mark that looked like a pig's tail.

Campanone, assigned to us as our school chauffer, took us and Fingers to town to show Jack where he could buy a briefcase like the one Fingers had that would be strong enough to sit on in an emergency. We weren't exactly sure what that meant, but we wondered about the fate of any briefcase that Fingers might own, since he weighed about 275 on a 5'5" frame. During the search for a store, the car barely missed a swaggering female pedestrian. Fingers let her have it in Spanish, which Jack interpreted as telling her she was going to get a dent in her chassis.

On a crowded street, there was only one way to park your car. You began by edging it into a space that was too small for your vehicle. Then you started pushing the cars in front and back of you back and forth with your bumper, until you had enough space for yourself. People were known to move a whole block of cars that way. The person parked at the end of the block set his brake so he wouldn't be pushed into the next street. If you happened to unknowingly park in an illegal place where everyone else parked, it was best to confess it to the officer who caught you. Truth would baffle him, and he would walk away without giving you a ticket. The school officials, however, had their own secret parking places when they had to resort to bribes in back alleys to get paperwork through.

Once all the trickery was over, we could concentrate on our jobs. The high school was housed in a large mansion, with the main offices located on the ground floor off a giant entryway, with a huge fireplace in it called an *hogar* in Spanish. Graciela once suggested that if our paperwork pile got too high, we could throw it all into the *hogar.* School trophies adorned the fireplace, and the school took great pride in showing them off. However, we discovered later that they also served as flower vases on Secretary's Day or receptacles for one-liter plastic bags of milk during lunch. During lunch in the faculty lounge, we were stared at by a cross-eyed, inebriated-looking wood carving of Abe Lincoln, after whom the school was named.

A large porch circled much of the mansion, wrapping itself around my corner office, which was spacious enough to house a couple of locomotives. A friendly coffee pot waited for us every morning, with coffee in it strong enough to make your eyes roll to the back of your head. Argentine coffee, mostly instant, was often served in tiny cups so you wouldn't eventually buzz out the window from an overdose. Over time, I finally convinced Graciela that she could make regular old American strength coffee. She felt badly about that, saying something like "Anita, I feel I'm making you deeshwater!"

Graciela was good about trying to keep me out of trouble. Once I talked about a woman who had an appointment to see me, commenting to Graciela in Spanish about the upcoming *mujer* (woman). She begged me to not call her a *mujer,* but wouldn't tell me exactly why. I figured out later, that in Argentina, it must have meant a woman of the streets.

The students' classrooms and bathrooms were all in the upper floors, and I was thankful it was no longer my job to patrol them. However, one time a teacher's grade book turned up missing. Of course I knew that missing grade books ended up in bathroom wastebaskets and on classroom bookshelves above eye level.

The school had an Olympic-size swimming pool and a large soccer field almost bordering the Rio de la Plata. Neither of the physical education teachers spoke much English, so our boys learned how to play all their sports in Spanish. I asked them later if they would understand the calls in English should they ever play in the United States. It really didn't matter, because if they were going to play another American School, they would have to fly to Uruguay, Chile, Paraguay, or Peru and be thrown together with a mix of languages.

I thought about the story of a Japanese boy who came to the States and regrettably found himself having to play high school football. His team members told him not to worry and explained which goalpost was which. All he had to do was to listen for instructions should he get caught with the ball. All efforts to avoid it failed, and as he stood there confused, someone yelled, "Tonyo, get on the ball!" So he put it down on the ground in front of him and stood on it.

Any boy who qualified for a major sport had to qualify for at least a second one to get the most out of the money spent on him to fly to games. David's main sport turned out to be soccer, where he earned the distinction of falling asleep once while playing goalie. Later a graduating senior willed him his pillow.

At the time, all three of my boys were built like matchsticks, and surprisingly, Dennis, the youngest and smallest, ended up playing catcher. That was quite a sight the day the students challenged the faculty to a baseball game. The faculty had no catcher, so they borrowed Dennis. They didn't have a pitcher either, so Jack mustered up the best of his high school pitching skills and threw to Dennis, who weighed about a third of what he did. Then on cue, the school nurse came out, did a heart check, declared Jack unfit, and placed a sign on his chest to that effect.

After Jack jogged to third base in the third inning, strange things began to happen. He would hit the ball, but someone else would appear out of nowhere to do the running. That paralleled his earlier life as a student, where his prowess on the tennis courts had resulted in more plays being wielded from a horizontal position than from a vertical one. It had earned him the fighting name of "Earthquake McGoon," a name which was to appear in any upcoming competition.

Of course Jack's chewing tobacco totally fit the occasion. A Mormon student sitting next to me in the bleachers thought it was funny that Jack was pantomiming all the spitting, until I told him it was real tobacco. His eyes opened wide, and he finally leaned back and said, "Well, it at least matches his shirt."

During a gigantic Buenos Aires all-school physical education gala event, David, who was the designated flag bearer for Lincoln School, was asked by an Argentine flag bearer what he thought was the worst swear word that an American could use. David paused for a moment, smiled, and said "Book!" The kid scowled at the grandstanders as he passed by, yelling "Book! Book!" He couldn't figure out why people were laughing and nobody was coming after him.

Only Jack and I knew why David's use of the word book was so funny, as he swore he washed his hands every time he touched a library book. He claimed the semester he got on the B+ honor roll, it was a total accident, and he'd see to it that it never happened again.

He did enjoy his music classes though, and before we knew it, all three boys were staged in a musical. Dennis played Kermit the Frog and captivated a little boy in the audience by his impromptu move of throwing a rose out of its vase and drinking the water. The little boy walked up to the stage stairs and sat on them, watching Dennis's every move for the rest of the performance. The frog horseplay extended on to some biology students, who later decided to put their assortment of pickled frogs in the faculty refrigerator for storage, which wasn't taken kindly to during lunch.

It was interesting to watch with whom the boys associated. Scott's friends seemed to be a mix of both boys and girls, most of them very academically inclined and ultra-friendly. David was into girls and dressed in his most zippy looking clothes, until he decided one day that he wanted to look and act like a hood. Unfortunately, he didn't have any skills for it. However, his black leather jacket wasn't worn out yet before he got over it. Dennis's best friends were missionary kids and bullies. He liked the values of the missionary kids, but understood so well what the bullies were going through in their lives, that they stuck to him like flypaper. If ever Dennis got challenged by a bigger boy, the bullies were behind him to defend him.

One boy really needed someone to come to his defense when the Americans were taken hostage by the Iranians, and that was our only Iranian student. Our worst fears vanished when we saw the other students come to his rescue and assure him that nothing was his fault.

My guidance office was a maze of student services functions, with a two-page, single-spaced job description for me. That meant I had to handle admissions, all registrar functions, financial aid applications, counseling, testing, student handbook preparation, personal evaluation of language ability, and placement into classes. Sometimes I even had to coordinate the curriculum. Students from twenty-seven nationalities were represented, which meant transcripts could come in from anyplace, translated or not. One Saudi Arabian student claimed that Egypt wouldn't send us his transcript because Egypt was mad at Saudi Arabia.

Our office not only served Lincoln School, but Argentine nationals as well, many sent over from the American Embassy. Most nationals tried to convince me I was going to get them scholarships to the U.S. so they could attend Ivy League schools. I finally had to put out a pamphlet, stating as nicely as I could, just what the pecking order was for admissions and financial aid. They weren't too happy to learn that in-state students came first, out-of-state students came second, Americans overseas were third, and internationals came fourth.

One young man even brought me a bribe of a pink sweater knitted by his grandmother, hoping I could move him up to first place. He wore it to our appointment in the ninety degree heat, so it wouldn't look like a gift to be averted by the administration housed in offices nearby. He took it off, failing to realize some amount of perspiration and underarm deodorant had clung to it.

Getting into an American college or university meant taking the SAT or the ACT, which brought in a plethora of long or unusual names, some of them too long to fit into the row of squares on the answer sheets. Names like Olsonoski, Yoshimura, Ichikawa, Luthard, Vasallo, Bonacorrso, Llull, Punzi, Bustamonte, Vandendreiss and Chiaraviglio. Once the ACT fell on the morning after the prom. Consequently one student was on the verge of falling asleep when a bird flew in. He couldn't take his eyes off of it and finally fell asleep face down on the mathematics section.

Ours was the SAT and ACT testing center for all of Argentina, as well as an alternative site for anyone else unable to take the tests in his or her own country. I had to be alert to cheating, as for some nationalities, this was acceptable practice. One girl combed her long hair down in front of her face, trying to hide her wandering eyes. I had to be especially alert with identical twins, who could exchange clothes during breaks. With them, I memorized warts, moles, bruises, dimples, scars, tooth alignment, drooping eyelids, and bad breath.

It was interesting to watch other cultural differences besides the ones related to test-taking. A Japanese freshman was so polite that he always backed out of my office when he left, which at least once, left the imprint of a file drawer handle on his backside. I would sometimes ask a student what had been the biggest problem in his or her home town. A boy from San Francisco claimed it was the old dead whale that washed up on shore and stunk up the whole metropolitan area. They kept towing it back out to sea, and it kept coming back again. Finally, they had to get some dynamite and blow it up.

A boy from Saudi Arabia said it was the airplanes, mostly Boeing 707s. He claimed that every time someone in his neighborhood bought an airplane, someone nearby had to outdo him and buy another one. I said, "I'll bet that sure made a lot of problems for the local traffic cops, didn't it?" Sure enough, the kid's uncle flew his own plane in for the boy's graduation.

Language issues sometimes took me by surprise. I almost got into some language difficulty when I had to help solve an Italian girl's problem in the presence of her mother, who knew only a little Spanish. Strangely enough, I could understand just enough of her Italian, and she my Spanish, that the girl only had to intervene a couple of times to get us back on track.

Another time I couldn't imagine why I was understanding a French woman so well, when she stopped me on the street to ask me if I knew where she could catch a taxi. It dawned on me she was speaking Spanish, but with a French accent. Once, a heavy-set oriental gentleman with a huge, round face came into my office. Somehow I expected Chinese to pour out of his mouth, but instead, I got a squeaky voice in Spanish, claiming his name was Delgado (meaning skinny). It's a good thing Delgado didn't have any bones to pick, because he could have sat on me and killed me.

School problems weren't our only concern. It would soon be time to start spending time noticing the issues of our growing teenagers. With puberty raging full steam ahead, David suddenly began making after-bedtime trips to the bathroom, which adjoined our bedroom via a very thin wall. We finally guessed that he was standing in there, waiting to hear something interesting coming out of our room. We'd lie there stifling laughter, until we could hear him finally give up and go back to his room. However, one evening we heard a big crash. While waiting, we figured he had fallen asleep standing in the tub and had taken the whole shower curtain and rod down with him. Hearing no cries for help, we played possum as if we had never heard a thing.

Dennis, on the other hand, would sometimes come into our room in the morning to see if we were still asleep. If it looked like we were, he often wouldn't notice Jack peeking and watching him flex his muscles in front of our large mirror. Scott was more of a loner, and was happy nestled in his tiny maid's bedroom, with its little half bath. It was okay, until big garden ants started coming into the house and running up and down his covers, playing with his hair while he was asleep, and examining the contents of his medicine cabinet. If puberty was giving him any fits, he kept it a secret.

David in parade
(first one in row)

Chapter 13

YOU WANT TO BRING THAT INTO THIS COUNTRY?

Since Jack had given up smoking in the late 60's and had taken up chewing tobacco, he ran into a problem. He had barely brought in enough chewing tobacco to last a bit beyond the arrival of the furniture shipment, not realizing the only tobacco chewers left in the country were the gauchos on the pampas. Otherwise, there were no stores for chewers and spitters because it was so socially unacceptable, and all attempts to find one failed. He put out SOSs to his brother and a couple of friends to send relief packages, and once when he was on the phone with his supervisor from Washington, D.C., he even asked him if he would drop Brother Doc a note about it. Later at customs, the postage plus bribes cost more than the tobacco did. In the meantime, we had to think up a ploy for getting a year's supply into the country in our ten suitcases each time we traveled on home leave.

If you got caught with a great amount of anything in your suitcase, you were accused at the airport of trying to set up a store, and your goods were confiscated. So we pulled a fast one and lined the bottom of each suitcase with pouches of Red Man. I would go through the line first, and when I was asked if I had anything to declare, I would smile and say in Spanish, *"Yes!* A whole *lot* of chewing tobacco." I would dig into the bottom of my suitcase, pull out a pouch, open it, smile, and offer some to the customs agent. His eyes would roll, and his nostrils would move back and forth like a cat sniffing a skunk, and he would let the whole family through without even looking down at our passports.

In case that scene failed, we learned I could put a couple of pieces of my dirty underwear just inside each suitcase. No inspector wanted to be caught staring at a bra and panties in front of 750 people disembarking from planes.

Another time we needed to buy new cameras, including one for our vegetable and meat store friends, whose money had been secretly tucked away under our clothes. With ten pieces of luggage, a box resembling a cheap wooden coffin containing two bicycle rims, and a used set of golf clubs, we figured we might as well get into the line for people with things to declare.

Unfortunately, things didn't look too promising, as our inspector acted like part Banty rooster, part spoiled four-year-old, and part Hitler, especially with four cameras hanging around our necks, two of them new and valuing over $2,000 total. Yet Jack may have had it all figured out that the box would offend the inspector's sensibilities, in that it didn't look like it was harboring an expensive TV and worth a large bribe - not even with my confession that we had a large supply of chewing tobacco.

Eyeing Scott's camera, he squeaked, "What do you have there?"

"A camera," said Scott.

"*Four* cameras!" said Jack, standing about a foot taller and a hundred pounds heavier than the little twerp with his possum-like nose.

"Yes sir. The whole family takes pictures," I had been primed to say.

Someone with some presence of mind handed him the oldest ones first, and after he snorted a couple of times, he said, "Hmph. Old cameras," and waived us on by.

Some new wrinkles presented themselves when we tried to get two stuffed birds out of Uruguay. I had gone with Jack to a professional meeting for South American school superintendents and had passed the time at a *feria* (street fair), where the natives were selling everything imaginable. I stumbled into a clever taxidermist, who had made a whistling heron look so real you would have thought it was alive. I bought the heron, along with a *bichofeo* (a name for the bird meaning ugly bug) like the one with an attitude who lived in our yard and thought he owned it, the swimming pool, and our two dogs. He had a beak like a woodpecker, which could sink deeply into dog flesh, a black and white striped head, and most of the rest of him was yellow. There were no sacks to put the *feria* birds in, so I had to carry them over my head through a tightly packed crowd. A gathering of small children started forming around me as I left the area, and I finally realized they thought the heron was alive and wanted me to lower him so they could pet him. I did and finally made it back to the hotel.

Once in a confined room, I suddenly realized from the smell, that the birds had been freshly processed. The only place to put them, without becoming asphyxiated, was the bathroom. I draped the heron's head over the toilet seat to make him look like he was hunting for a fish. Who cared what the maid thought.

Fearing we might be challenged at customs, I lined the bottom of a carry-on with dirty underwear and placed the birds down inside, with their heads and half of their bodies sticking out. The Uruguayan inspectors were so thrilled we had bought something in their country, they just laughed. The inspector at Ezeiza airport didn't think it was funny, but didn't challenge us. The problem came trying to get them home. The heron looked so real, that no taxi driver wanted him in his vehicle. The twelfth driver finally accepted us after I kissed the bird on the beak to show he wouldn't bite.

The heron story continued even after we got back to the States. When we unpacked him in January, it was bitter cold and windy. The movers had carefully protected the birds using little Styrofoam balls. However, the box came apart while the movers were unloading it, and static electricity took hold. Little white balls stuck like glue to the movers, the van, and to everyone's vegetation within a three house radius. I thought I would never get them off myself either.

Later I was asked by the elementary school special education teacher to come tell the class about Argentina and to bring something from there. So I brought the heron, who in the process of being petted, dropped the last Styrofoam ball from under his tail. The kids were dumbfounded as to how a dead bird could lay an egg, and nothing I could say would convince them otherwise.

Much later, after being on display in my office for several years, the bichofeo's head finally fell off. The heron's underpinnings started weakening, until his beak was eventually resting on my fake praying mantis. Sadly, I laid him to rest.

The plane ride home our second year consisted of a 747 plane load of unsupervised, having-been-to-Miami, screaming, misbehaving, Portuguese teenagers festooned with Mickey Mouse hats, peacock feathers, cowboy hats, tight jeans, radios, and you-name-it. Their guides were of the same ilk, only twenty-five years older. Since this was our first time to be routed through Caracas, Venezuela, we were looking forward to buying something in the airport. We were at the airport about three and a half hours and never left the plane.

The two tour guides who were leading the pack were supposed to get off at Caracas, as they were discount passengers, so that two paying customers could get on. When the pilot began paging one of them, they hid. Four men in suits got on and started combing the aisles. Then the police got on and did the same. Soon the kids started screaming and shouting, a couple of them crying, and a near riot broke out as time dragged on and the airlines couldn't get the problem resolved.

The temperature inside the plane soon rose into the nineties, and Jack cautioned the stewardesses that if someone didn't get to a decision pretty quickly, they would not only have some physical encounters, but some medical problems. Fewer than five minutes later, a boy passed out from the heat and had to be carried off. Finally the two women were forced off and left, screaming and beating on the walls of the plane, threatening lawsuits. The kids refused to quiet down for a time, so the plane couldn't take off. Jack and I stood up and stared most of them down into their seats, until the plane could finally take to the air.

Once we thought we were going to have trouble getting Dennis out of the country two weeks ahead of us so he could go to Boy Scout camp before our regular home leave. The problem was that he needed the signature of his real father on a certain document, stating he had permission to leave the country. That being impossible, we lined up any document of his that we could find in both languages, dressed him up in a suit, and waited with him in line along with his two brothers, so it would look like the whole family was going.

When he got to the window, he handed the gentleman his flight ticket.

"*Documento*?" the man requested. With an air of confidence, Dennis handed him his birth certificate in English and no telling what else. The man glanced at the documents, looked at the size of Jack, and waved Dennis on through.

Jack almost got into it on one flight, when he didn't realize a short Japanese fellow had gotten in ahead of him in the men's restroom. Thinking the room was empty, Jack thought the door was stuck, jerked it even harder, and finally kicked it with his foot to see if he could budge it loose. The door finally opened, and he was met with a string of Japanese blasphemes that would turn a turtle blue. No amount of apologies could stop them or the evil looks that went with them, even after the fellow finally sat down right in front of him. I posed the question, "Don't you think you'd act like that too, if some giant had tried to break in on you in the middle of doing your business?"

Culture shock overseas could almost be matched by culture shock going back and forth on home leave. I asked a man on the plane what time it was, and he pulled out his pen to look. A store clerk wondered what planet I had come from when I stared in disbelief at a ball point pen containing erasable ink. I thought an Anthony dollar was a quarter, until I got sassed by a pop machine. On the other hand, since I had to buy such large quantities of things to take back to Buenos Aires, my shopping cart brought on remarks. An old gentleman, who had been watching young girls in the candy section, noticed my twelve cans of Spray and Wash and commented, "You must have a *lot* of ring around the collar." Since I often shopped for Argentine friends, I still had to collect twelve cans of hair spray, thirty pairs of hose, four tubes of denture adhesive, five vials of bee sting medicine, and two flea collars.

When a cashier at Wal-Mart asked me what in the world I was going to do with thirty bottles of liquid paper, I told her I was going to drink it. Then I handed her a 10,000 peso bill, which made her go stiff. She finally muttered, "I can't do this," shaking it as if it were crawling with fleas.

That gave me an idea. I tried the peso thing on the shoe repair man, this time with a 300 peso note, which by that time, wasn't worth much at all. He thought it was so funny, that I gave it to him. The following Sunday, I put a 10,000 peso note in the collection plate, and judging by the stares as it went down the aisle, I could tell someone was figuring on building a new addition to the church. I thought of a check I had written to the church a couple of years ago for our monthly pledge. Under the place where it said *memo,* I wrote in "For sin and riotous living," just to see if anyone at church was paying attention. No one said a word. Maybe they were afraid to. But a month later, a laughing bank teller called me.

Aside from trips home, one of the most memorable plane rides within the country was taken by Jack and Scott to Ushuaia, the southernmost inhabited city. The seniors had opted to go there for their senior trip and had asked Jack if he would go along as one of their chaperones. The old WWII C-47 plane loaned to them was crowded, because it was partially loaded with machinery parts, so they had to make two separate trips. By the time Jack and Scott arrived, there was quite a bit of snow on the ground. They were still able to take a side trip to the waters bordering the line between Chile and Argentina, where some trouble had been brewing. They saw a ship from each country menacingly facing each other, each no bigger than a destroyer escort.

Scott was unaware of the warning not to take any pictures of the warships there, and got his film confiscated when he took one. The rest of the students were in a nearby building staying warm, while Jack was outdoors making snowballs. Suddenly a guanaco, or wild llama, confronted him, and Jack, thinking he might catch him, made a lunge for him. He spit all over Jack's glasses, who decided that was grossly unfair. Since he had a mouthful of freshly chewed tobacco, he unloaded it all over the beast until he ran out of tobacco. They both fell in a snowdrift, and the animal ran off, leaving a cluster of students to steam up the windows laughing.

Guanaco that spit on Jack

Chapter 14

WOULD YOU LIKE A CHEW AFTER WE KISS? AND OTHER STORIES

We were unaware there would be so much kissing going on at school, or any place else in Argentina for that matter. Once you knew someone for any length of time, maybe even a couple of minutes, you got kissed when you left and kissed when you came back. Not the good old slurpy kind, but kind of a cheek-to-cheek thing with a little noise you were supposed to make in the right ear.

I don't know where all that came from. Maybe from the sweet and loving Italians when a lot of them fled to Argentina during World War II and started marrying the Argentines. Or maybe it was the Germans when they fled for the same reasons. By the time the custom had spread like wildfire, students and faculty were kissing each other, faculty kissed faculty, and everybody kissed the high school principal. You didn't even go to a professional meeting somewhere else in South America without being kissed by another colleague.

I thought it was pretty nice, until we got to a professional meeting in the States, where some of our South American counterparts were. We had to stop short for fear our American friends would wonder what the heck had been going on in the bushes behind our school. A missionary kid found himself in about the same fix when he was on home leave with his parents and was introduced to a foxy-looking blonde. After he kissed her goodbye, she slapped him, saying "Do you go around kissing every girl you meet?"

The faculty at Lincoln School wasn't used to some of our ways either, especially when it came to new inventions. The boys brought some erasable-ink pens back to their teachers, and one of the science teachers was so enthralled with his, he wore the eraser out during his free period. The boys knew he would be the most captivated by it, as they had already watched his colleagues pull fast ones on him in the cafeteria. When the science teacher asked Tony the math teacher if he knew how hot it was outside, Tony looked at his watch and told him. A few minutes later, he thought there might be a storm brewing and wondered what the barometric pressure was. The other math teacher looked at his watch. The science teacher finally blurted out, "You have all those instruments in your *watches?"*

Besides being an excellent science teacher, this gentleman always wanted to make sure his students were happy. When it came time for the prom, he would single out a boy and ask him if he had a date to the prom. If the answer was no, he would pick out a girl and ask her. If he got the same answer, he would brighten up like a lit Christmas tree and say, "Then why don't you two go to the prom together?"

We became great friends with Tony and his wife, Carola. Tony liked calling Jack *"El Bufalo,"* and when they wanted to have us over for dinner, Tony's classic phone invitation was, "Your house is surrounded! The tanks are outside!" Once when they were all over at our house, we had the additional pleasure of Carola's parents as guests. They were part of the German community populating Cordoba in northern Argentina. Jack almost got lost trying to keep up with stories in three languages, but did pick up quite a bit about the sinking off the coast of Uruguay of the WWII German warship, the Graf Spee. On a trip there later, we were fortunate to have a taxi driver take us to the very spot and tell us the story as he had actually seen it as a kid.

Eating together at school was also a bit unusual. The Armenian typing teacher had the most interesting fare: spinach, rice, vinegar and oil, or maybe eggplant, tomatoes, lemon juice, beans, and raisins. A history teacher, for all practical purposes, was on Weight

Watchers, except for the time Jack tried to accuse her of eating frozen gorilla pancreas. Most all were yogurt addicts. To the widowed music teacher, a meal could be made out of a whole bag of marshmallows or several apples. Sometimes he would sit and let his stomach growl, hoping someone would leave him something extra that was home-cooked. We could always go back to our restaurant fare school lunch program of steak, pork chops, chicken, or ravioli, but too much good food made us look like blimps.

Once a year, we quit drinking milk out of the school trophies and got them ready to use as flower vases for Secretary's Day. That day was loudly announced in advance by one of the secretaries, until you began to think it was the upcoming birth of Jesus with firecrackers to help celebrate it. If I remember correctly, that was the only occasion in which the honoree didn't have to provide the refreshments. Otherwise the custom was for the feted to bring the birthday cake or whatever to the rest, which I thought was a trifle unfair.

These folks were used to unfair, having lived most of their lives under a dictatorship.

However, living in a dictatorship was one of the most unusual things we had ever experienced. The military junta that had taken over had succeeded in almost completely eradicating a fierce reign of terrorism, using a technique that said that if you even wanted to act like a criminal, you could be made to disappear. Consequently countless lives that could have been lost at the hands of terrorists were saved, but some innocent ones were lost in the process. That set off an unresolved stream of human rights criticism and dismay in both Argentina and the United States.

Reality proved that we could now safely walk the nine blocks from the train station to our house at 2 a.m. and never worry. With rare exception, our neighborhood was crime free, nestled in a metropolitan area of fourteen million. Another big issue came up when we caught one of our American students with drugs. Drugs were unforgivable in Argentina, and the police were primed to make drug offenders disappear if they were discovered. So Jack took a leap of faith and took a translator with him to the police station to ask them what he should do. Totally cooperative, they told him that if he could have the boy out of the country in twenty-four hours, they would leave him alone.

Other school issues were much less harrowing. The American School was essentially treated very kindly by the Ministry of Education. The elementary and junior high school sections were still under its jurisdiction, but the high school came under the jurisdiction of the U.S., the Southern Association of Colleges and Schools, and was associated with the Department of State in Washington. So it pretty much had free reign, and as far as the Ministry of Education was concerned, to the tune that we could have been manufacturing girdles in that building.

When we first came, the only perceived school problem for our boys occurred with Dennis, who was still in junior high, and who had to begin classes both in English and Spanish, without knowing a word of the latter. It wasn't long before I saw a Spanish social studies book lying around, and I quizzed him about how he was getting along. I hadn't realized he was being totally immersed, including on the school grounds and after school watching Spanish TV. Almost all of John Wayne's old westerns had been converted into Spanish, and since Jack had most of them memorized from back home, he was learning more Spanish than he would ever admit.

Early on, Jack gave up taking lessons in Spanish, because he just didn't think it was right that he should have to say "dog black" instead of "black dog" and let a foreign language screw up his brain. So he learned to pantomime almost everything he wanted. I told him he'd better learn how to tell someone he needed to go to the bathroom, or he'd be up a creek. He agreed, as long as I would teach him how to order a beer.

At the local train station, he had quite a system, using only one word to get his round trip ticket to Retiro station in the Capitol. He would hand them the right change so they couldn't cheat him, point his thumb in both directions to indicate a round trip, and say "Retiro" to indicate his destination. After that, he would sit quietly in his train seat, chew his tobacco, and spit in the bushes when he got out.

Once Dennis went with him and decided he wanted to mimic his stepfather, so he asked him if he could have a chew for himself. Unfortunately, he needed to spit before they got to town and mumbled something about where he could do it. Jack told him that if he wanted to be a real man, he was going to have to figure that out for himself. Jack discovered that when the train stopped in Olivos, Dennis was gone. Frightened, he started looking for him and found him barely holding the train car door open, where he had slipped out between the cars to spit on the loading platform.

Dennis wasn't the only one intrigued by the tobacco. Jack's secretary wanted to give it a try, but Jack discouraged her for fear she would throw up in his office. Someone tattled and said she eventually chewed some anyway when he wasn't looking. The campus security guard watched the tobacco scenario for days, but never did understand Jack's pantomimes indicating you were supposed to spit it out. When he finally tried some, we didn't see him again for the rest of the day.

Jack was always afraid he would run out of chewing tobacco before time for our home leave to the States, so he put his extra packets in the freezer so they wouldn't mold. The only other means for bringing in tobacco might be to ask any scheduled visitors sent by the State Department or the Southern Association of Colleges and Schools to bring some with them when they came down for meetings. He finally had to give up that thought and be satisfied with the stories they brought instead.

One member of the accrediting team of the Southern Association of Colleges and Schools told about the time he got hung up for three hours in outer Atlanta, Georgia, traffic due to the overturning of a huge truckload of pigs while he was trying to get to the airport. The Georgia Highway Patrol was all out in hot pursuit, trying to tackle the pigs around the middle so they could tie them up with their belts, a rather dismal scene at best. A second committee member finally got tired of all the stories and the long, drawn-out evening meeting and fell asleep, hitting his head on the edge of the chair next to him as he toppled over.

Every day in Argentina seemed to put us into a new world and me further into the dictionary for more technical language. Soon after we first got there, Jack had desperately needed a haircut. He had watched me cut the boys' hair, but decided he wasn't ready yet to risk it himself. It reminded him too much of the time he had tried it on his own boys. When he had finished cutting, he had marched them all to the barber shop and had asked the barber to finish the job and please keep his mouth shut while he was at it. Superintendents got enough bad press without becoming an item of gossip in a barber shop.

I took him to the only Argentine barber who had been recommended. A beautiful, slinky girl gave me a cup of strong coffee before she led Jack behind a dark curtain, presumably to wash his hair. I didn't hear any screams, but had to wait awhile before Jack emerged with his hair fashioned like a lion's mane. When we got back to school and told the principal what it cost, he said, "Good grief, did you pay for a haircut, or did you pay ransom?" After that, it took a good pair of scissors and the dog shears to get rid of the mane, and when he discovered I was well worth the money I wasn't getting, he let me have the job.

There were a few other things we had a hard time locating, even though getting around in our own suburb to buy food wasn't a big problem. If we wanted baking soda, we had to go to the pharmacy, and popcorn had to be bought at the pet store. While we were in there, we snooped around at the parrots, but found out there might be a better deal at some strange location north of us. I couldn't believe I actually got up at 6:30 on a Sunday morning, drove to a canal to buy a shivering parrot out of a box from a disheveled-looking Argentine lady with a cigarette hanging out of her mouth, and the thing wasn't even interested in biting me.

I took him to a waiting cage in the car and took him home, where we found he was still so young he hadn't learned to climb well enough to keep from falling off his perch. He would ask for things by bleating and barking like a dog. He ended up sampling apples, potatoes, gold wrist watches, ears, drapes, and furniture and tried to eat his water dish. Sadly he didn't live long, partly due to our inexperience, so we went for the pet store variety. Our second one was a contortionist and liked to hang upside down and look at us from between his legs. He enjoyed dancing to the Tijuana Brass and sitting on my shoulder while I fixed breakfast, combing my hair with his beak and bracing himself by sticking a foot in my ear.

If we wanted any more animals, we had to be satisfied with watching the outdoor or indoor wildlife. That started with the cats that frequented the food stores, often with their own places staked out and fiercely defended. Some had real jobs, like the bean inspector in the rotisserie shop. Strangely, the cats in the fish stores ignored the fish, but concentrated on sniffing purses and nylon hose.

Giant sized *cucarachas* (cockroaches) that came in under the back door were not quite as welcome. At least we seldom saw them until we turned on the light at night, and there a dozen or so of them would be, almost an inch long apiece. Our resident *bichofeos* kept the mole grasshopper population outdoors down and us amused by dive-bombing into the pool after insects, or by taking a bath suspended in mid-air. Once I tried to show a *bichofeo* how to make pancakes through the kitchen window, making him crane his neck and stand on his tiptoes so far that he almost fell in the pool.

When it came to medical needs, we were fortunate in finding excellent doctors. They took more of a holistic approach, which probably explained why there was an unusual abundance of psychiatrists. However, many Argentines, who couldn't figure out what was wrong with them, would blame it on their livers. This included symptoms ranging from long-term runny noses, to stomach aches, to arthritis, to poor vision. Duke was beginning to have some trouble with arthritis, and his vet had been selling us some tremendously effective medicine. I commented to the vet how nice it would be if Jack could have something that effective for himself. So he wrote me out a detailed prescription formula in Spanish for Jack to take back to the States. I questioned how an American pharmacist could understand his Spanish, but he assured me it would be no problem, as it was all Latin-based.

Once I had a runaway bladder infection, so that my dictionary and I had to be taken to the German hospital. We all had to struggle with Spanish as our second language, but in the end, they came up with a diagnosis that nobody in the States had been able to pinpoint. I got wonderful treatment there, including a Christmas program held outdoors for anyone who could be possibly moved, bed and all. I had a little trouble hearing the music, because a senile old Spanish-speaking German was reciting poetry in Russian, with a voice like a buffalo. Someone finally poked him in the ribs, and he quieted down. Even the birds were friendly. One came to the window every morning for breakfast, and a dove tried to get in under the window during supper. I'd never had to wolf down hospital food before, for fear a bird would get it.

Jack had already put braces on the teeth of his three teenagers and now was facing another three. Scott didn't need any, but David and Dennis did. The recommended orthodontist was Dr. Festini, whose office was within walking distance of our house. Once the boys were fixed up, Jack took a second look at my teeth and told me what a raving beauty I would be if I could have mine straightened too. That had been a thirty-year dream of mine, not to come true, as an orthodontist told my mother I could never have braces without further damaging a front tooth already damaged slightly during childhood. Dr. Festini's specialty was adult orthodontics, and after one look, told me he could do the job with no danger to my affected tooth, which he merely ground down a bit. Although I wasn't concerned about braces on my teeth at 42, Dr. Festini kept showing concern for my social life, as well as my threshold of pain. He planned to put as few bands on my teeth as he could and wanted to see me once a week.

The little brass wires first used to separate my teeth wouldn't have been so bad, had I not had to attend the annual reception and buffet supper of the Saudi Arabian Ambassador and his wife, the parents of two of our students. I looked like I had fish hooks in my mouth and resembled a camel eating a tree. Then came the curiosity of the next smile. Did the fish hooks look like they had been baited with bacon, turkey, fish, prune skins, parsley, or pea hulls? Ordinarily, to cover sharp wires, orthodontists used wax, but unfortunately, the only wax in Argentina for braces was bright red. If your smile got into the red zone, you looked like a vampire or a hemophiliac. I think some of Dr. Festini's fears about my reaction to it were confirmed, when I accidentally bit him on Tuesday, September 22.

The red wax did have its advantages. Parents sympathized, stating they hoped I would get well soon. When I went shopping, I could get almost anything I wanted by just smiling and holding out money. Once I had a flat tire on a busy street, and when I smiled and asked the nearby gas station attendants if they could fix it, they couldn't get to it quickly enough. Nobody who didn't speak English wanted to stick around a middle-aged woman with braces on her teeth who looked like a vampire in a fur-trimmed coat.

After he put an appliance in my mouth to split my palate, I did the supreme act of stupidity by trying to sing a solo in church. I started out, "Duh Lord iss my schlepherd, I chshall not want….." When Dr. Festini heard my confession about my sloppy singing, he started telling me about his blunders learning English. He was in a class learning about words that were opposites. He was extremely timid about speaking up, but when the instructor asked for the opposite of the word, freeze, he jumped up and shouted, "Antifreeze!"

Jack had always wanted braces on his teeth, but his parents couldn't afford it. When he saw mine were doing so well, he asked Dr. Festini if he could do anything with his, especially the front ones. The only option seemed to be that of pulling out Jack's two front teeth and replacing them with a bridge. Dr. Festini thought about that for awhile and finally announced, "Meester Allman, yoo haff great beeg overlapping teeth in dee front and I wood haff to replace dem weeth leetle teenie teeth. Dat wood geeve you psychological problems, so I theenk we better forget dee whole theeng."

Life did move on in spite of any medical issues. Right before his first big date to the annual Southern Star Ball, Scott took a terrible fall while he was looking after the *asado* and came in confused, bloody, and looking like a duck-billed platypus. A quick hospital visit got him all patched up, but later Jim eyed him and said, "My gosh, Scott – how are you going to kiss her with that fat lip?" As usual, Scott took things graciously, even the ribbing he got earlier from his brothers when he lost his class ring and found it hours later in his undershorts. They thought it was so funny they started calling him Old Dead Butt.

Jim had originally come just to visit us after he graduated, after finishing some long-awaited traveling overseas. He planned on staying for only a couple of months, but soon gave serious thought about finding work in Argentina. He was in no hurry to go back to the States and find himself a bride, claiming he wanted to sow his wild oats until he was thirty and then get married. When that finally happened a few years later, he married a cute school teacher named Susie and they made up for lost time by having twins, Sam and Ben. In the meantime, a teaching job in a nearby Argentine school came up, and while Jack was in the States at a professional meeting, he brought Jim back a handsome suit to interview in. When he came over to our offices to show it off just before the interview, he solemnly asked, "Have you got a good funeral I could go to while I'm all dressed up in these clothes?"

Jim got the job after interviewing for only thirty minutes. A month later, after he got his first paycheck, we caught him sitting on the floor and counting out hundred dollar bills with the most astounded look on his face. It sure beat minimum wage in the States. Later we were fortunate to have Jim around when the maid broke her arm. We paid him to do the housework, which he cheerfully did until he got to Dennis' room. We overheard, "Dennis, why am I finding library books in your dirty clothes hamper?" Once he came downstairs and asked me, "Do I *have* to clean under Dennis' bed?"

Dennis, in spite of his small size for awhile, turned out to be the chief translator for Jack and his stepbrothers. When Jeff came down for a visit, it was like Mutt and Jeff all over again, with Jeff being over a foot taller. Dennis wasn't about to let anyone take a nickel off of him; in fact, he wouldn't let people off the hook if they tried to cheat any of the family men out of money. Their size and his mouth always won.

He won again the day we came home from school, and an old bum had decided to take a nap under a tree in our front yard. Dennis woke him up and started telling him some things even I didn't understand. The bum looked horrified and took off. Dennis never would tell me what he said. After that, if anything needed fixing, we usually called in Dennis who would find some way to get it done, even if it was unorthodox.

Toward the last, the Argentine economy was quickly going into a slump, and things within the American School were showing signs of political unrest. People earning American dollars were being replaced by those earning only pesos to get them cheaper. Jack felt it might be in our best interest to start looking for jobs in Missouri and even leave in the middle of the school year if we had to. When a job came open in Ava, Missouri, he took it, and we prepared to say goodbye to some dear friends and a country we would never forget.

Calle Nueve de Julio

La Casa Rosada—The Pink House instead of the White House

Sports Palace, Luna Park

Jim and Jeff
Allman

Chapter 15

WE KNEW YOU WEREN'T FROM HERE

We were about to encounter quite a challenge when we moved back to the States in January of 1982. The only Missouri opening in midyear for a superintendent of schools was in the small town of Ava, located in Douglas County. The natives called it Booger County, claiming that's where all the boogers came who were trying to hide in the mountains from the law. I wondered what we were getting into, especially since the last superintendent had died on the job, and most of the rest before him had been fired. Knowing some of this, Jack's buddies called him up the first day of school and asked him where they could send his welfare check.

Nevertheless, we were warmly greeted. I arrived a week before the rest of the family and stayed with some generous school people so I could buy a car and some furniture to furnish the small three bedroom barn-colored house the carpentry students had built. Jack had only seen the inside of it by the light of a cigarette lighter when he flew home for an interview. It was plenty adequate for Jack and me, with only Dennis remaining at home.

Scott had already gone off to college, and we had left David in Argentina to finish up his senior year. His friend Gabriel's family offered to keep him, none of us realizing that swords were rattling and the Falkland War was about to break out. The argument raged as to whether the islands were called the Falklands or the Malvinas, and the Americans just wanted to stay out of it. The Argentines were disappointed that the Americans were backing off from taking their side. Some considered it a slap in the face and started giving Americans the evil eye. Consequently some capitalist-type Americans fled to Uruguay, and many avoided speaking English in public. That worked for David, as he looked more Argentine than American anyway.

We started watching the news like vultures over road kill and making periodic phone calls to the American Embassy and to the school to make sure David would be safe. In the long run, he claimed that the only thing that got in his way was the peace-making Pope and his huge crowd of followers when he came to visit Buenos Aires, thus making David late to the senior prom.

When we finally picked up David at the airport, we were surprised at some of the reverse culture shock he was experiencing after living only one semester with a Spanish-speaking Argentine family. It was mostly English words and phrases he was fumbling for, which I understood, as four of us at one time or another had to revert to thinking in Spanish while we were living there.

David went on to live with his father for awhile, and Dennis got ready to finish his sophomore year. I told him his bedroom would be his own private domain, as long as he kept it clean and nothing fishy was going on in there. I reserved the right to occasionally deep clean it, with the promise to keep out of his desk and dresser drawers. That worked just fine, until one day I saw fruit flies crawling out from under his door. Some of the lunches I had fixed him, so he wouldn't have to eat school lunch, had been laid aside so he could spend his lunch hour chasing girls. He had hidden them under the bed so as not to disappoint me, and fruit flies were hatching in the apples.

Since students at Lincoln were so much more advanced socially and academically than most American kids, Dennis thought sophomore girls were immature and silly and immediately began dating a senior, who was delightfully funny and a good match for him. His attraction to seniors continued, when one named Wes came over to the house to welcome us soon after our arrival. He and Dennis became fast friends, and in the process, we learned Wes and his family had a pet monkey. The monkey mostly stayed in the house, but one day he got loose out in the yard about the time a truck-driving drunk pulled up in the driveway. Wes and one of his friends went out to see who it was, followed closely by the monkey, who jumped up onto the hood of the truck and started grimacing at the guy through the window. The drunk hurriedly got out and backed away, screaming, "Somebody help me! There's a monkey on my truck!" There was silence. "Can't you two see it?" he yelled again.

"I don't see any monkey," said Wes, trying to keep a straight face.

"I don't either," said the other guy.

A few years later, Wes showed up as a student at Missouri Southern State College where I was working as a counselor. He'd been working for the Joplin police force and decided to finish up a bachelor's degree in criminal justice. He'd drop by my office from time to time and give me a big hug, almost always wearing his bullet-proof vest. I wondered about that, but was afraid to ask. Before he finished with the police force, he went undercover to hunt for drug offenders and crooks and had to dress up like a thug. He grew a beard, let his hair grow long, took fewer baths, discarded his deodorant, and wore dirty clothes. One day he went back to Ava to visit his folks all dressed up like that. They didn't recognize him and wouldn't let him in.

The furniture wasn't due for another six weeks or so. We were lucky to have made enough money from the sale of much of our furniture in Argentina to buy what we needed until the rest got there. I wondered how many inch-long Argentine *cucarachas* would be waiting to run out of the boxes. Once there, the movers weren't sure what they were up against with box labels being in Spanish. I'd get questions like "Hey, lady, what's *ropa*?" Misconstruing the purpose of our dictionary stand, the same one yelled, "Where do you want your pulpit?"

There was no teaching job for me when we got to Ava, so I tried substitute teaching for the first time. What a switch from being an assistant principal in charge of disciplining students, to this – a bunch of kids with their own lesson plans on how to conjure up trouble with substitute teachers. Luckily these students were great kids, and I only had to drag one chair outside the classroom so Mr. Cute Stuff would have no more audience than a row of lockers and an occasional student walking by.

As to study hall, I became a bit worried about Rob, who wasn't getting anywhere. By eighth grade, he already weighed 200 pounds and wore a one inch thick plastic chain around his neck. Fortunately they finally sent him off to a learning disabilities class. I thought maybe the chain around his neck was keeping blood from getting to his brain. One other student discovered he wasn't going to win any prizes by writing a note to a second student making references to his study hall teacher as a scum-licking maggot.

While I was substituting, I started my correspondence courses in geography. I waded through Japan's rice, Africa's diseases, India's emaciated cows, Russia's names which all sounded alike, China's yak milk production, and the ravages of the boll weevil in North America. At the last minute, both the students and I were saved, and a job teaching Spanish and one class in psychology became available.

Some students were under the misconception that we had lived our whole lives in Argentina, making us some sort of a mysterious oddity to be admired. I let them quiz me about our background, surprising them that we had only lived there three and a half years. "We knew you weren't from here!" claimed one of my Spanish students, who slumped down in his chair to demonstrate what he thought he and his peers were like.

Others didn't know Dennis had a different last name and assumed Jack was his real father with whom Dennis had some secret and privileged school connection. Sometimes he would hear, "Go tell your father that................."

"You can go tell him yourself. His office is right over there."

My classroom was on the second floor of an old building whose staircase went up and down with you when you used it. To stay fit for those stairs, I signed up for an aerobics class, taught by a wonderful P.E. teacher, who pretended she didn't notice the bad shape I was in, nor that I couldn't get my rear up off the floor. After all, my greatest physical exercises had consisted of childbirth and housecleaning, and the thought of doing anything that would make me sweat gave me cold chills. I hated going up and down those stairs, huffing and puffing like I was being chased by giant lizards. I had yet to look forward to menopause with all its electric lights. So far, my skirts with their elastic waistbands were even giving up on me. My metabolism was heading south and I was growing extra parts.

After over a year of exercise on a hard gym floor, I was never so glad some years later to be able to switch to a water aerobics class, even if it was at the city pool, which had twigs and grasshoppers in it. There I wouldn't have to sweat, and no one would laugh at you unless your swimming suit was ripped.

Since my Spanish classes were small, I decided to invite each class over to the house for an Argentine meal of *empanadas*, but only if I could get some help chopping onions. For every pound of hamburger that went in, two pounds of hand-chopped, cooked onions had to go with it. That meant waiting until we could go outside to do it on a day the wind was blowing toward the neighbors. The empanadas went over so well, that one kid forgot and ate the toothpicks holding his together. A second ate so many that he had to disappear temporarily. I figured he was outdoors throwing up in the Pfitzers.

Teaching a pretty great bunch of kids was the fun part. However, in spite of many nice people to work with, Jack found some serious problems with his job. Someone hadn't gotten the message that bus drivers were not supposed to own their buses, nor be allowed to *sell their routes* to someone else! That made the hair on the back of Jack's neck rise. It was alleged that the bus drivers pretty well ran the school anyway, which was highlighted the day Jack got a call that a bus driver was going to come to his office and kill him. A board member on a party line in the country had overheard the conversation. Jack went home and got the axe handle he'd kept behind his desk in Joplin. After notifying the sheriff, he put a gun in his desk drawer that his oldest son, John, had sent him.

Jack's experience with bus drivers in general had been pretty good, except for a time in another superintendency when he had to fire one for insubordination. When Jack and the chief maintenance man went out to the driver's house to pick up the keys and the bus, the man refused to give them to him. For the first and only time in Jack's career, the argument regrettably ended up in a fist fight, which Jack didn't want any part of, but not before the driver announced that Jack could stuff the keys and the bus up his rear end sideways. The man finally threw the bus keys at Jack and then screamed at his wife to get the shotgun. Jack and the maintenance man jumped into the two vehicles and hastily took off. Years later, when Jack was at Joplin, he found out the bus driver had gotten saved. The driver didn't know how to get ahold of Jack to apologize, so he apologized to the whole congregation, stating the whole thing had been a setup between his boy and him to get Jack mad enough to get him out to their house so they could beat him up.

Later when Jack and I were talking about all this over Saturday lunch at the local restaurant, we overheard a conversation between two men about a local murder case that might not get solved because, according to them, someone had lost the bullet. Things were obviously escalating beyond Jack just having to confiscate Monday morning porno from third graders on the school bus.

The porno raids reminded me of a story told by a first grade teacher. One of her students showed up unexpectedly early to school. Suspecting something, she asked the little girl if she'd had breakfast. When the answer was no, she took her out and bought her some. Finally she quizzed her as to why she had come to school so early.

The answer wasn't pretty.

Chapter 16
DON'T QUIT NOW

Our stay in Ava was shorter than we expected, as Jack fell into the same trap as his predecessors and couldn't dodge the school district's tendency to fire superintendents. Now he had to think about what to do next.

For some time, Jack had dreamed about eventually retiring and returning to his home town in Anderson, Missouri. Our income in Argentina was almost twice that of what we'd been making in the States, so while we were overseas, we decided we could afford to purchase some land and have a home built there while we were still out of the country. We drew up the house plans, made arrangements with a contractor, and the next time we returned to Anderson on home leave, we started picking out everything from faucets to roof tile. That was some feat, since we only had one week to do it. At the time, we weren't sure when we might return to the States, so we asked our friend Kenny and his wife, Myra, if they would like to live in it and take care of it for us, which they did for two or three years. Kenny was an Anderson barber and farmer, later to become the county assessor. He was so funny that you never knew what was going to fall out of his mouth. Myra was a great homemaker, so between the two of them, we knew everything would be well cared for.

Later we asked them to have someone finish the rooms in the basement, so at least we could temporarily have two rooms and a bath to ourselves should we come home before they could move out. At that time, Kenny quipped, "Maybe we could rent those two rooms out for one-nighters until you get here. Over here in this unfinished part we could.......uh, sell.......uh....... sandwiches and uh, ...wieners and uh ....*oxygen*!" Kenny had already told one on himself before he and Myra moved in, trying to explain why they had to buy a whole new bedroom set for upstairs.

"Myra and I had gone to bed and were busy having our monthly, when the whole bed fell in," he said, with a red face. "I just said, 'Myra, don't quit now!'"

In the summer of 1984, we had to tell Kenny and Myra we needed to move into our house. Issues weren't quitting there either. I had landed a job at the high school teaching Spanish, psychology, and sociology. Before I got started with that, there were some changes that we were going to have to consider due to some carpentry misfires on our otherwise beautiful home.

The place in the bookcase for the TV had been erroneously built to extend into the room so it looked like an upright coffin. A strip of wallpaper was missing from the bathroom, and the water wouldn't stay in one of the tubs. A screen door had fallen off, and something mud-colored had bled through the kitchen paint. Air conditioner piping overhead was fashioned so that water drainage had to run uphill. Then when I looked through the peephole in the front door, I realized it had been put in backwards so the burglar could see in and we couldn't see out.

The house got sold that Kenny and Myra were planning to rent before we got back, so it took awhile for them to find another one. In the meantime, he told Myra, "I guess we could go live in a school bus." That wasn't too far-fetched from what was going on south of the County anyway, and it reminded me of a story my friend Brenda told me.

Brenda had an old relative in Hot Springs, Arkansas, whom she had not seen in years, so she and her three kids decided to try to find her and pay her a visit. She finally found her living in an old caboose in the woods that she had made into an apartment, and when Brenda approached it, she noticed the door wasn't hanging on too tightly. Brenda was a spotless housekeeper, and already things weren't looking up. When she went in, she was warmly greeted, and quickly saw things were in a mess. She balked over the thought of the sanitary status of the refreshments, but ate them anyway. When she headed for the bathroom to wash her hands, she found the tub was being used to store empty boxes. When she returned and sat down, she heard the door squeal, and in walked a goat.

"Don't worry about him, honey," she said. "He comes and goes whenever he wants."

As Brenda was leaving, she noticed her relative's old Jeep sitting in the weeds close to the house. One of her girls had whispered that she had seen the goat sitting in it and putting his hooves up on the steering wheel like he was driving it. "Do you drive that very much?" she asked.

"No, honey," the lady replied. "The goat ate the front seat, and it's so low I can't see out."

Evidently he wasn't the only local goat that got into it. An older lady, living not too far away, had gotten all dressed up in a beautiful flowered dress to go with her family to a nearby petting zoo. A lethally friendly goat decided it was lunch time, and when she wasn't looking, started eating her dress.

Before they moved out, Kenny congratulated us all for living so successfully with each other for those few weeks, quipping about how proud he was that "no one went to bed with the other guy's woman."

Anderson seemed rife with local color, so I started paying better attention. It had no courthouse, so there was no place for old men to hang around and chew the fat and spit. Because of the fire that wiped out the competition, it was down to one grocery store, where there always seemed to be a very colorful, self-appointed weather announcer. He was one of several different people, but usually wore an old hat, a coat that was too long, and overalls. He frequented the front counter, often carrying a loaf of bread and a can of dog food. He was wired for sound and could be heard clear back to the eggs. He announced floods, snow up to the eyeballs, insect infestations, and tornados.

The other place to go for reunions was the drug store, which was also the Bible shop, gift shop, and book store. Charlie, the pharmacist, had everyone's prescriptions memorized, which came in handy one Sunday morning when an older lady had a spasm in church.

If you got in a jam, there was always someone to help you, who knew more about your car, septic tank, dog's dose of worm medicine, furnace filter size, or heart condition than you did, and usually had something in his trunk to fix it. If he couldn't fix it, his father-in-law could.

Back in the classroom again, I hung up the poster Dennis had given me during his senior year in Ava, showing an old gorilla scratching his head and saying "I'm Too Smart to Study and Too Cute to Care." I got out the textbooks that I didn't like and prepared to come up with some of my own tricks, starting with the Spanish alphabet. That was easy to learn, and in a day or two the students could use it to spell any English word they wanted and make it look like they were Spanish wizards. I had to laugh at one of the girls who said, "It's so much fun being a freshman where I can say dumb things and not care."

I tried to keep up their interest by teaching them some extra silly words to use as substitutes for the ones in the text. For example, they could practice translating sentences like "My mother talks to my father," and then substitute with "My mother spits on my father," and think they'd pulled a giant fast one. When Halloween came, I gave them a whole list of optional gory Spanish words to use on their siblings.

No matter what I did, one boy finally succumbed to the "no falling asleep in class" rule. The first time that happened, I sneaked up on him and dropped a heavy Spanish dictionary on the floor beside him. The second time, I let the class all sneak out when the bell rang, leaving him there to wake up in my psychology class. He woke up halfway through it, and when he saw what had happened, he hurriedly put his head down on his desk again to save face until the next bell rang. He mumbled as he left, "I'll never do that again."

To get them into writing Spanish sentences, I divided them up into groups and let the groups invent stories about a wandering goat. I suggested they use their imaginations as to where the goat went and what he did, like boarding an airplane, wandering into local stores and a couple of churches, eating the flowers in the cemetery, or trying on clothes. One student got caught up in the clothing thing and the next day looked up at me and announced, "You've got thirteen sweaters!" I wondered how he might be associating that with the goat, but I didn't ask.

Teaching psychology and sociology was more fun for me, because Anderson was a small town, and I could throw in some local color. When we got into the chapter on social control, I asked them who they thought were the worst gossips, men or women. After a lively discussion, I finally challenged them to look into the local coffee hangouts and then decide. They all agreed it was the retired men. Some of the women would confess to gossiping, but the men swore they were just gathering information.

In psychology, when we got into the chapter on sensation and perception, I suddenly had an idea. I asked them if they would be willing to see what it was like to be without sight and to see how their other senses kicked in when that one was missing. Half of the class volunteered to be blindfolded during our second lunch shift and to eat lunch that way, as long as another classmate accompanied each blindfolded student to make sure he or she didn't fall down stairs or get into any danger. They even had to go to their lockers and try to get their things ready for their next class. We extended the lunch hour so they could get back to class a few minutes before the end-of-the-hour bell rang.

They pooled their scarves and bandanas, and soon students and teachers from other classes were coming to their doors, wide-eyed, as the class went downstairs to the cafeteria. I ate lunch in our classroom to keep out of their way. When they came back, it was total excitement. Many were moved at how eager others were to help, including showing them how to help themselves. Even more amazing was their awareness of sounds and conversation around them.

The next day, the other half of the class begged to be blindfolded and try it too. Although each had been assigned a partner, one girl came back, blindfolded and alone, with everything in her locker ready for her next classes. When I asked her about that, she explained that if this were real life, she would have to do it by herself and she wanted to see if she could.

Almost every second semester, a new kid would show up in sociology class from California or New Jersey and would attempt to make his mark in class by loudly proclaiming his agony over the culture shock. I quickly learned to find something positive within each of his semi-disruptive statements and to ask the students what they thought about that part. It was part of my strategy to help him feel accepted, not only by them, but by me.

Expecting some sort of a prank to eventually evolve out of that, one day I pretended I didn't feel a light touch on my back as I went down the stairs to the cafeteria. When we came back, just outside the classroom door, I pulled off a sign that said "Kick Me," which I had purposely left on all during lunch. Then I looked at the class and said with a big grin, "I want to congratulate the person who was clever enough to put a 'kick me' sign on my back without me knowing it."

Of course all noses pointed to Mr. California, who, after he finished blushing, grinned sheepishly, and said, "I knew you would be the only one I could do it to that would laugh and take it right."

My last year there, I had to teach one geography class based only on the two geography classes I had taken by correspondence. I warned students in advance to try to escape and take the other geography teacher instead, but twenty-five or so victims ended up in my room. When I learned I would be expected to teach German by satellite the next year, without knowing a word of it, my search for a counseling or an administrative job stepped up drastically.

For over a year, the McDonald County R-I School District had been running without a tax levy for reasons a sane person wouldn't want to hear. Consequently a lot of the high school roof leaked, as did most of the school roofs in the rest of the county. One of the biology teachers warned me that if it rained real hard, I would see Muscovy ducks swimming on the roof outside my window.

Some water was already leaking into the back of the room, so I put a big rain bucket under the leak. I opened my door some time before first hour class started, so some freshmen boys, not yet ready to chase girls, would have a place to throw spit wads for target practice. Before the first year was out, I asked one of them if he weren't about ready to comb the halls looking for a girlfriend. He decided he would, but came back with his handful of wads, claiming there wasn't anyone out there he'd have.

It was no small feat to take control over the neckers and the smoochers, some of whom sat on the radiators to do their performances. I didn't think that was doing the plumbing any good, so I finally asked the principal, at what point did he want me to put a stop to it.

"When they're tangled up like worms," he said. So with the business teacher on one end of the hall and me on the other end, both playing Attila the Hun, our second floor hall was fairly well cleared of problems.

Our house was on a hill overlooking the high school. It seemed a waste of gas, when we could almost swing from a vine to get to work. We could see all but about twenty percent of the countryside, giving us some spectacular views of sunrises and sunsets, as well as gorgeous fog scenes. I stayed camera ready for five years, capturing God's beauty every few days, no matter what the season.

On a night I was to take tickets for a basketball game, I could see a super sunset brewing, so I headed down the hill early to see if I could get a picture of it setting behind the big statue of the school's mascot, a black mustang. After three tries, I realized I was going to have to lie down on the parking lot to get his full silhouette, unless I just wanted to see his ears. I imagine that scene created a few rumors the next day as it went around school. It's a good thing I had learned to do the silhouette thing, as every year, the graduating seniors painted the mustang's private parts red. Since I was prone to entering my photographs in contests, I figured judges wouldn't take too kindly to the full view version.

This seemed like the right time in my life to get into some other things for myself as well, so I started up woodcarving again, something I had learned in Ava. It all started when I saw the need to keep our friend Fred off the streets in his retirement years. Fred certainly loved to be a part of the card gang when it met in the basement, but occasionally he would have fits and yell and swear and throw his cards all over the room. About the same would happen to his golf clubs, so that someone would have to go around and collect them out of the bushes.

With all his pent-up energy to spare, I figured it was time to gather Fred and some more friends together and offer them all a free class. Fred gave the whole thing a suspicious eye, saying he didn't want to get involved in making any silly wall plaques. So I invited him over as an observer only and laid out a pattern for me to do of a head of his favorite dog, a Labrador retriever. He was hooked. He started on that same pattern and was well into creative genius, until he got to the dog's nostril. The more he carved away, trying to achieve perfection, the bigger it got, until a wren could have made a nest in it.

He called me up one day to tell me that woodcarving was ruining his life. "I can't smoke 'cause the ashes fall off and burn the wood and I can't drink 'cause it makes my hands shake," he griped. In spite of his ruined life, he kept carving and got so good at it that I don't think even he believed it. Some time before he died, he gave me a beautiful carving he had done of a butterfly, one of several he had finished and given away.

Soon after the wood carving started, I decided to write music. Jack was in the hospital suffering from some kind of undetermined lung ailment that didn't make his prognosis too promising. For some reason, at that most depressing time, I got out my little portable organ and church music poured out. That was no small task, as I had only taken six months of piano in the seventh grade. I stuck pretty much to hymns so I wouldn't have to figure out any runaway accompaniment. I imagined that some day I might take that up again, but 1987 was the last time I was depressed. So I reverted to concentrating on our dogs.

Our dog Duke had died from cancer and old age while we were in Ava, and it was time to get a partner for Spot before she got too old to enjoy it. She was used to staying within the perimeter of the property, which would be helpful in training a new pup. So we bought a Labrador pup and named him Charlie. Of course Charlie had to do his puppy thing and got into the garage and chewed up most of the pictures from my first wedding. What upset me the most was the one of me in the wedding dress I had worked so hard to make. My only solace came when I found a duplicate set among Mother's things twenty years later.

Once Spot got Charlie trained, she started to get pretty tottery and one day disappeared. We feared she had crawled off to die, but three days later, we started looking for her, on the hunch that maybe she'd fallen off the bluff behind our house. We took the truck around to the bottom of the hill, and carrying a blanket with us, started calling for her. Pretty soon we heard a whimper and looked up to see her caught in a tangle of branches about two-thirds of the way down.

It took Jack awhile to get her out. We gathered her up, put her in the blanket hammock-style, and carried her to the truck, where Jack put her in my lap. As he started up the motor, we looked into her face and saw big tears starting to stream out of her eyes. We had never seen a dog cry, and it moved us to tears too. We took her home, where she was barely able to stand up and eat a little food and drink some water. She lasted another three months, until one day, she could no longer get up, and we had to take her to the vet to be put down. We buried her on the property, just like we had done with Duke in Ava.

Her presence was temporarily replaced by a neighborhood stray that first appeared at our friend Basil's house, part of whose property we had bought to build our own. This dog had the intelligence of a gnat, and no matter how many times Basil told him to "git," he never would, but would instead get closer each time. Basil finally figured out that the dog thought "git" was his name.

Jack didn't know it, but he was in for some serious back surgeries and he had almost waited too long to get them. Along with several disks that were obviously in trouble, some stenosis in his spine had caused some of the nerves to bind together, causing another painful problem. He had taken two months out of his early retirement to go to Texas to help start up a couple of business schools, when it all came to a head. He ended up in Tulsa, where he underwent two spinal surgeries, and came home to begin what was supposed to be a long recovery.

Not too long after that, the McDonald County Schools called him, saying they were going to need a new superintendent around October, and would he be available. What a dilemma! He had always wanted his last superintendency to be in McDonald County, as he had wanted to give back something in return for all the good things he felt he had received there. He thought a long time. Then he decided that if he had enough strength to go down to Main Street and heckle his friends over coffee every day, he had enough strength to go back to work. So two years after I had started there as a teacher, he came on board as the superintendent. Friends came streaming in, bringing congratulations, bouquets of flowers, plants, black carnations, and sympathy cards. That was at least one step better than what had been done to the superintendent before the last one who had lived in the city too long. That one thought he was being honored, when some of the locals sent him on a snipe hunt for them.

Jack had enjoyed his friends' coffee house stories and would miss them. One friend had told about a funeral in one of the small towns east of there. It was a military one, held under a canopy in the rain, with hardly enough dinky little wooden chairs to go around. The deceased veteran's little boy was being cared for by the veteran's mother, a large woman who was holding her grandson in her lap and having trouble sitting in one of the chairs. Finally the muddy ground gave way under her at the moment of the gun salute, and she and the little boy toppled to the ground. With her breath knocked out of her, the woman couldn't get up. Suddenly, without thinking, the boy jumped up, and after an inappropriate outburst of profanity, he screamed, "They've shot Grandma!"

About the time Grandma was being shot, I decided it was time to see if Southwest Missouri State University would let me finish the series of counseling courses I had started at MU, so I could complete my counselor certification. That would have to occur in several stages, beginning with summer school. Since the campus was seventy-five miles away, that meant I would have to stay there during a couple of summers and come home on weekends.

The only viable place for me to live was in an old, reconstituted hotel called the Kentwood Arms someone had turned into a dormitory for older, expired students like me. I had to figure out how I was going to do my cooking in one room and a bath and soon discovered that if I ran the coffee pot and the toaster on the same circuit, it blew out fuses on practically the whole floor. So I had to set up the coffee pot in the bathroom, which meant I had to be very careful where I stepped. At least it was quiet there, which was not the case the next summer, when I had to live in a brand new dorm containing incoming freshmen going through orientation, some not completely removed from the smoke bomb mentality.

My roommates in an adjoining bedroom to our common kitchen were a mother and daughter combination, whom I enjoyed immensely. We were all on the alert for younger student pranksters and didn't have long to wait before the fire alarm went off. We soon discovered that we older students had no sense of reason when it came to such things. We erroneously concluded that it might be students setting it off on purpose and spent too much time deciding just how we should appear as we went down the fire escape. Should we put our bras on under our pajamas so as not to appear too risqué, or should we just flop our way down to the bottom? The second time, I suggested that before flames started licking our feet, we might want to hurry up the job. Someone else commented that if we got in too much of a hurry, we'd end up with our bras on backwards. The third voice said then we wouldn't know if we were coming or going.

That eventually led to a real concern about a young, black man who was spending too much time watching the residents on our floor come and go and would stand by the elevator and wait for women to get on so he could get in and follow them for a ways. That got pretty spooky, until finally I told the woman in charge of the dorm, that if this and some of his other strange activity was going too far, I would write up a report and sign my name to it. I knew any other woman would be too scared to do that. In the meantime, I went over the man's records with her, and learned he had been dropped at the dorm by his parents and no one seemed to be able to find his home address.

At 11:00 p.m. the night before finals, she came to my room and nervously asked if I could write the report for her, which I did. Two women came to me the next morning and said someone had gotten ahold of the right authorities who came and got him and escorted him off in a straight-jacket.

As it turned out, I wasn't the only one who wanted to go back to school. Unknown to us, Jeff's nearly completed business major hadn't exactly been his cup of tea. Under his bed in his trailer was a stack of English grammar and literature books revealing his true passion. It didn't take long for us to convince him that he would be welcome to come live with us in Anderson while he finished an English education major.

That put him in close proximity to where he and an old girlfriend had dated heavily, but with whom he had long since broken up. We asked him why that hadn't worked out, and he claimed he had given up women because all they did was take your money and play with your head. We found out later that his true love was Maxine, back in St. Louis. After he finished his degree, he went back to her and finally settled in as an English teacher at a mostly minority school in the inner city.

As Jack got deeper into his job, some of his problems were escalating. One evening, he came dragging in, saying, "Someone tried to shoot a school bus."

"What in the heck for?" I asked.

He explained that some kid's younger brother had been kicked out of school, which ticked him off. So when the school bus came down the road toward his house, the kid got a loaded shotgun and ran after the bus while it was making its next three stops. As soon as he could get close enough, he started shooting it full of buckshot, tearing off leaves and tree limbs and scaring the bus driver and all the kids.

Another night, Jack came home with a bit of a blank look and that shall-I-quit-before-it's-too-late-face. "Would you like a kiss?" I asked.

"Only if you'll keep the voltage down," he said. He waited a moment to get his breath. "For the first time in thirty-six years, I had to suspend a student for breaking wind," he sighed. I couldn't stop laughing. I thought of the pizza, brown beans, and prunes that had been served in the cafeteria one day, with no hope of opening the school bus windows in sub-freezing weather. The kid had allegedly been eating too many beans at breakfast every morning, so that by the middle of the morning, he was able to cut loose in class. By noon, when he went to the cafeteria, he could very well orchestrate it, much to the amusement of the students. No amount of detentions, suspensions or anything else seemed to stop him, and it finally got to be a daily classroom and school disruption, which at this point was a legal case for the final expulsion.

The story didn't end there. The kid's mother came to school to announce that her son had every right to pass gas if he wanted to, because it was healthy. She demanded a hearing with the Board.

They set it up, and she and some of her relatives stomped in. She started to plop herself in Jack's chair, when someone indicated a seating section they could have. She went through the same song and dance with them, until a Board member finally got up and said, "That is *enough!*." No one was quite sure where the kid went after his final expulsion by the Board. He must not have left a trail.

PART III

Chapter 17

MSSC AND RETURN TO LEARN OR SOME SWORE THEY WERE BRAIN DEAD

It was 1988, and I was about to start my eighth new job as an educator at age fifty. My resume was beginning to look like I could never hold a job. Jack was two years away from retirement, and I had just slammed the door on teaching, or so I thought. I was now at Missouri Southern State College in Joplin, starting my first day as a counselor and academic advisor and teaching an all-morning class of scared spitless adults coming back to school. It was a college orientation class called Return to Learn, and I was supposed to make them feel comfortable and convince them to graduate.

I had already returned to school seven times myself and was slowly becoming a student addict and a fixture at two universities. At that, I needed credibility, as I had never been a counselor in the States, and my last college job involved spying on druggies and trying to catch evil-doers.

My past history didn't matter to them. All these students wanted was for someone to care about them and to help them get through school. They came with so many insecurities about their abilities, stemming from childhood abuse, lapse of time between high school and college, recovering alcoholism and drug abuse, age, brain cells they'd figured had melted, early marriage and childbearing – you name it. One claimed she had spent twenty years raising children and said she just wanted to be around someone who knew the whole alphabet. She even thought about becoming an orthodontist so she could get her money back.

In every class, I started the first day by putting all of our chairs in a circle. I encouraged each one to tell a little about him or herself, but I always started the dialog to give them a format for sharing. I included things like my early and current family life, what prompted me to go to school, how I came to decide on a major, and things that still concerned me. No matter what I told them, I always topped it off with how sad it was to have to go through a divorce, and that soon afterwards, my ex-husband married my sister. Then I let them off the hook with body language so they could react or start laughing.

"Good grief! How can we top that?" one asked.

They figured if their teacher could go through that and confess it to a crowd on the first night, there wasn't anything they needed to hold back. There were stories, tears, laughter, and the most incredible bonding, so that by the time class was over, they didn't want to leave, and I wanted to take them all home in my truck.

Their stories over the years were awesome. One had fallen off a water tower, and another wanted to major in criminal justice because she was tired of making toilet seats. Another gal said she wouldn't marry a certain fellow unless he quit drinking. He did, but still chewed. She wished he didn't, because she didn't want to marry him without a bottom lip. One woman's husband was still in jail, and another claimed her brother was a lunatic.

A man claimed he'd wasted away the best years of his life, had been arrested in foreign countries, and had a sister who collected husbands. He was under forty and had a pacemaker and was soon to have his fourth hernia surgery. He refused to miss class after the last surgery was over, so we dragged a couch into the classroom and laid him out on it. After an hour and a half, he turned a bit green and went home.

A younger fellow bought a mule because he missed being drunk and had a sister who married his second ex-wife's first husband. One in his mid-thirties came to school because he was sick of raising cows. A quiet, funny lady claimed she was dull and her parents were even duller because they were dead. Nobody believed her about the first part. The woman sitting next to her said her father sired thirty children and remembered all of their names. At 70, he had a six month old child. The lady quipped, "He's an all-star player!" The woman said her father wanted to retire.

"What from?" the lady asked.

The last time one woman saw her son, he was handcuffed and boarding an airplane. Another lady remembered me from my Joplin High School days, when I carried around a six inch ruler to measure skirts. More than one person came from families so dysfunctional that they had to raise their parents. One girl started to cry when it came her turn to share, because of the awful life some of the others had experienced. She felt bad because hers had been so good.

Almost everyone was petrified of math, and several women were or had been truckers. A middle-aged lady raised llamas and spun her own yarn. Once she mixed some with twenty percent dog hair, which she got from a friend after she'd had her fluffy, white dog groomed. Many women had husbands who were threatened by the thought of their wives going back to school, thinking the wives would get ahead of them or be hit on by other men. One gal came to school to be moral support for her friend. The friend didn't finish, but the supporter graduated with a nursing degree five years later.

"Your mom should marry my dad," a woman said to the man next to her, after they had told about multiple parent divorces. One girl had married at fifteen and was divorced by seventeen. A young man claimed he really didn't want to work or get up. When he told about a big party he'd thrown, a married couple across the room suddenly realized their daughter had been to that party. Later another young fellow claimed he was secretive and boring and sped off on his motorcycle, never to be seen by us again.

After I gave a pretty sophisticated personality inventory to the class, where everybody could read everybody else's results if they wanted to, three women got onto a fellow named Bob, claiming that "surely you aren't like that!" Bob came to my office the next day and asked me if I would change his personality to get them off his back.

One group concentrated mostly on their pets. A young woman told of her cat that had died, whereupon she wrapped it up in her fur coat, secured the coat and the dead cat with duct tape, and called in a backhoe to dig a grave. She brought in pallbearers and a preacher for the funeral.

I was busy in my office when one of the other counselors came to the door to announce there was a woman outside who wanted to enroll in my fall class. She was a truck driver, wearing a witch's type black hat, was chewing on a toothpick, wearing a muscle shirt, and had a belt on with a large buckle that said, "How is Your Peterbilt?" I knew this was going to be a challenge when she showed up to class wearing another muscle shirt that said, "All This and Brains Too!"

Her vocabulary in class would have made the hair stand up on a meerkat, which somehow merited her neither dirty looks nor applause from the rest. The next week, she had changed into a more subtle brown hat, was wearing an attractive pink sweatshirt, and had dropped most of the profanity. She announced she had been told she was too dumb to go to school by every agency imaginable and that she was here to see if she could make it in college anyway.

The class members were all asked to write a two-page composition, and hers came in eloquently describing a place where she shouldn't have been and properly using some pretty big and appropriate vocabulary words. The only word that was misspelled was Jacuzzi, which told me she had spent quite a bit of time using the dictionary. I could tell she had some writing talent that just needed some direction.

She was eventually tested, and told us she was thrilled to find she had a learning disability and wasn't dumb at all. Along with her

English emphasis, she tackled a foreign language, and needing a study partner, paired up with a young man aspiring to be a minister. By the time she neared graduation, her thought processes had completely changed and she was conversing with me with all the genuine enthusiasm of an English teacher.

Sue, once an alcoholic, became such a wonderful worker and trusted friend that Jack and I eventually hired her to occasionally work for us at home. We finally gave her our house key, as we had so many different things for her to do, from my parents' bookkeeping, to pet care. It also let her stay at our house from time to time and take a break from family life with kids and grandkids while we were on vacation. The pets loved her, but it was sheer devotion to take care of them, since the parrot bit her a couple of times, just to prove he was king.

There were countless success stories. So many had come to school thinking they were brain dead. They took catch-up classes in English and math to make up for lost years in high school, only to find themselves later teaching other students in the learning center or working in our offices. Many were invited to join the freshman honor society, and an occasional one received the prize for being the best student in his or her department. Some went to work for the very agencies that had pulled them out of the dark holes of their lives. All they needed was some encouragement and some strategies for helping them realize where all their negative self esteem issues had come from and how they could turn that around into something positive.

One day I thought about my mother's "Can you think of any reason why you can't...?" approach. I knew if I tried that with these adults, they might come up with some dark-looking lists. So I tried something else like it that I had learned in one of my education classes. I started asking them if they could think of anything for which they had absolutely no choice.

"I can't choose not to pay taxes," one said.

"You can't?" I asked.

"Oh."

Another said, "I can't choose to walk naked down Range Line Road."

"Really?" I asked. Couldn't you choose to, but you don't because you don't want to face the consequences?"

"Yeah."

Pretty soon it got really quiet, until some woman said, "I can't choose to be a man."

I said, "That's a good one, although some have tried to mess with that." That led to the conclusion that we really can't change most of the events of our birth like sex, eye color, and so on. Then the inevitable came.

"I can't choose when I'm going to die, because God is going to choose that."

Pretty quickly they saw that the second thing you couldn't choose was *not* to die. I eventually tried that in every one of my classes, and the only two things the classes could think of for which they absolutely had no choice were the events of their birth and the fact they couldn't choose not to die. Only one time did a student come up with a concept they couldn't quite resolve, which was the idea that we couldn't choose how we were raised. That led into a long and complex discussion.

However, with the power of choice at their disposal, I began to ask them questions such as, could one choose to be happy? Or could one choose to give out one's best effort toward being successful? Or could one choose to abandon some of his or her upbringing and learn new behavioral and self-awareness skills? Then I would guide them into another exercise I'd learned; how to determine what percent of success is skill versus what percent is attitude. It was an attempt to lead them to the results of a study showing that eighty-five percent of success is attitude and only fifteen percent involves skill. Once we finished that, I'd ask them, "So what are you doing here in college if only fifteen percent of success is skill?" They didn't know how to answer that, but suspected I had something up my sleeve.

Every semester in each class I gave my dress-for-success speech, emphasizing that at any time, a future employer might be watching them. The next week after one of those, I noticed how nicely dressed one class was. "We want an A," one of them said. Later when I gave that same speech in one of my Career and Life Planning classes, one girl took it almost too seriously, coming to class in a near-ballerina outfit. A fellow in the same class insisted that what a person wore on the outside wasn't a reflection of the inside. He lost his argument, when it slipped out that he hadn't gotten a job because he wasn't dressed properly for his interview.

An elementary education major came into my office one afternoon, blubbering because someone in the department had gotten onto her for wearing a Mickey Mouse shirt. "But I want to relate to the kids!" she howled. After all my speeches, she still went away unconvinced.

Another had a confession to make to the whole class a few weeks after one of my clothing lectures. She had washed and dried her clothes the night before and had hurriedly reached into the dryer to grab a sweatshirt and put it on before rushing on to class. When she got to class, she pulled off her coat and sat down, only to discover at the end of the period, that one of her very large bras was static-clinging to the outside of her sweatshirt, out of her sight under her boobs.

One woman was especially interested in learning how to dress, as her mother had spent a considerable part of her life under a bridge with a six-pack, never even talking to her daughter about personal hygiene or menstruation. Unguided, she had turned to drugs, but now was on the road to recovery. She claimed her son, however, was enrolled in college in Springfield, majoring in girls and bars. Another woman lacked so much parenting that she clung to me like flypaper. When she started following me to the bathroom every day, even a long talk went unheard, and we finally had to ban her from our office area until she got the message.

A middle-aged gentleman had spent years as a successful construction worker, not knowing he was schizophrenic and wondering why he kept hearing voices. By the time he was diagnosed, he was nearly homeless, and when he got to my class, he was living in his truck. Good medication was working and life was moving forward. One day someone in the class asked him what he was going to major in. He put on a sly grin and quipped, "I'll do whatever the voices tell me."

One young woman came to school with a confession that she had been terrified of people for a good part of her life, and if it hadn't been for empathetic personnel in high school, she never would have graduated. She wanted to go to college and wondered how she could do it. I told her we could put her chair by the door, so if she felt she needed to escape, she could do so, and I would act like she was merely dashing off to the restroom. Not once did she have to leave. Next semester we secretly notified her teachers of her dilemma, who planned the same strategy.

Before long, we needed an extra student teacher to help teach a freshman orientation class. On a hunch, I asked her if she would be willing. She thought for a moment and then said yes. She did a marvelous job. Over three years after I retired, I ran into her working as a nurse in a Joplin hospital. She had changed her major more than once, but in four months, she was going to graduate with a nursing degree.

She was one of many whom we called "stop-outs." They came to school for a time, then stopped out for various good reasons, then came back again. For a few, it took twenty years to graduate, but it was worth it.

There were others I wished had been in this class. One class member took a delightful, but heavily tattooed and pierced young man under her wing, hoping the attention she gave him would allow him to quit bidding for it by wearing a pencil through his nose. Another came to school all beaten up and with a concussion and finally had to drop out. This was the second husband that had done that to her.

Many, both in and out of the class, were adult children of alcoholics. Some weren't aware of it, but as they told their stories, all the symptoms became evident. Low grades and failure to succeed in school were other tip-offs. Some we chose to dismiss from school until they could get on their feet with professional help; otherwise, it was useless to take their money.

In addition to students in my classes, I had an extraordinarily large amount of advisees and counseling clients. Since our counseling and testing department was in charge of quite a number of those who had yet to decide on their majors, many often reeked with indecision. One man already had a successful career as a surveyor, but wanted to change to something else. It was not only taking him months to decide what, but to even organize his thinking. Finally he told me he bought Ogilvy's book, *Living Without a Goal* and then confessed he lost it in his house somewhere. When he finally found himself, he made such a comeback, that during the last semester before he finished his bachelor's degree, he ended up teaching one of the classes he was supposed to be taking.

I had three questions I would ask undecided students that seemed to point them in the right direction more than anything else. First, what would you really like to *do* (not *be*) every day that would really make your eyes light up? Second, what's keeping you from doing it and how can you overcome that? Third, what do you want to learn?

One fellow didn't get past the first question, when he told me that he wanted to sit in a chaise lounge by the ocean drinking a martini. He was about thirty-five and wearing a gold necklace. One of my colleagues had always claimed those types were undoubtedly in crisis. This student didn't realize how much he was telling me. I said, "I sense you would rather be somewhere else other than here. Like living by the ocean doing something that would really be fun."

"You're right."

"Then why are you here in Missouri?"

"My grandmother is paying my way for me to go to school."

"What are you thinking about for a major? I asked.

"Business," he replied. "My grandmother thinks that would be a good one."

"OK. But I don't see your eyes lighting up. Now tell me what you would really like to be doing for a living, if nothing were in the way of doing it." Then it all poured out. He wanted to teach people how to water ski. He longed to have a little store near the ocean where he could sell refreshments and ocean-related beach-type recreational equipment. He was eager to show people how to be safe when they were just playing out in the water. Pretty soon he saw how a business degree wasn't so bad after all, but he needed more.

He, along with others searching for their dreams, had a chance to be rescued by a degree we called the bachelor of general studies. It really wasn't a general studies degree at all, but one with strict rules about the basic core and upper division hours and other things. It allowed a student, with proper advisement and administrative and committee approval, to combine two or more disciplines, so a person could meet his or her goals in life and maybe even do the unusual. It was really a bachelor of individualized studies degree.

It gave one young man in the EMT program a chance to consider his dream of mountain rescue. Little did he know that I had recently talked to two Canadian ambulance drivers about this, as we sped from Banff to Calgary, Alberta, with Jack lying in the back. They had told me all about the crazy folks on vacation who thought they could leap the Rocky Mountains with a single bound, but who instead fell off bluffs and into ravines and thickets in the freezing cold. Shifty, suspicious animal eyes would look at them, and noses would snort steam into the air, while fearful people with abrasions and broken bones would have to wait for someone to notice their disappearance and call for a rescue team.

In addition to their medical training, these two skilled, young men knew three languages apiece and all about animal behavior involving beasts with horns and furry things with warring teeth and claws that might get in the way of a rescue. They knew some geology because they had slippery Canadian slopes to climb up and down, and some meteorology because they always had to know what the weather was going to do. The young man sitting next to me was amazed and thought ahead about the business classes he might also have to take in order to go into the rescue business for himself.

A young lady, who was already in the dog grooming business, was surprised that I didn't think that her vision of owning a high class dog boutique seemed trivial. I already knew an art major who knew so much about iguanas, that the local veterinarians were consulting her and having her draw up information pamphlets. What would it take for a dog boutique? Animal science, psychology involving animal behavior, business classes, and maybe even a photography class. Why the latter? Because if a person were going to spend that much money getting a pet beautifully groomed, why not get a good picture at the same time?

I worked up other programs like horticultural therapy and daycare operation for students changing their minds about continuing in the education program. One advisee wanted to become a writer and blend English, psychology, and philosophy. Another wanted to own a ranch in Montana, and the student sitting next to him wanted to do everything involving airplanes, from flying them to maintaining them. He was tired of his mother suggesting he should become an accountant. It wasn't long before all sorts of students with this special degree were walking across the stage to receive their diplomas and get on with their lives.

Along with some other familiar faces, I kept seeing an older gentleman in the halls on our floor. I never knew his major, but I found out he wasn't willing to give up, even when he found out he had an incurable illness. Day after day, he helped tutor students who were afraid of math and science. I watched him as he worked with them in the library, patting their shoulders or stroking their hair like a kindly father. Then one day, I saw him struggling up the stairs with an oxygen tank. He passed away before he made it to graduation, but he had achieved the greatest goal; that of helping so many others get to the finish line.

Our oldest graduate at the time was a widow in her seventies who had already been to junior college. She asked if she could live in the dorms, and she was granted the privilege. She begged the students there to treat her just like they would treat each other. "Oh no. We've got to do better than that," they said. Near the end of her schooling, she found she had cancer and was ready to drop out of school. Her communication department advisor wouldn't think of it. When she went across the stage in a wheelchair, she got a standing ovation.

Chapter 18

THE WHITE-HAIRED IDIOT

Nobody had warned me about the hazards of upcoming technology when I was in graduate school. In fact, I was a semi-idiot when it came to anything with or without wires attached to it.

Back in 1991, I was the designated testing administrator for the senior exit exam (ACT COMP) for the students in the School of Technology and the School of Business and I had really done my homework for this. To house that many students, we had to put them in an auditorium and in two large classrooms one floor below. I was the only person reading the instructions, so this involved an intricate system of proctors, timers, microphones, control room operators, runners, and such. Since it was a timed test, if a student threw up on his test from eating too much breakfast with sausage and bacon, it meant all sites had to shut down at once and resume when ready.

They handed me a walking microphone – a first for me, so I could move around and also be heard in all three rooms. No sweat. Things went off like clockwork. During one of the longer test segments, I slipped back to the control room, covered the mike with my hand, whispered to the professor in charge that I needed to use the restroom, and would he please step up front for the three or four minutes and proctor.

Whistling, I tripped down the hall and banged the usual bathroom stall doors. I started the first wrestling match with the panty hose.

Suddenly I realized the microphone was still on. All sense of reason totally left me. Standing there with my thighs pinched together with ripples of nylon, I finally woke up and flipped off the switch.

When I returned, the proctoring professor had disappeared. Another grinning one was in his place. The test-takers were busy, unruffled, and harboring no silly looks. Good, I thought. The mike was too far away. Just in case, not wanting any scores to be affected, during the next segment, I stepped out into the hall to report it to the chief testing official. She started laughing and said she was going to report me to ACT as an aberration. Seconds later, a criminal justice professor came up from one of the rooms downstairs and loudly said, "Gads! I knew that microphone was sensitive, but I didn't know what we were getting into!"

At lunch, I asked an English professor friend what everyone had heard. "Oh, it wasn't that bad," she explained. Now what exactly did *that* mean, I asked myself. Finally the vice president for academic affairs came up to me, shook my hand, and cracking up, said, "Congratulations, Mrs. Allman, you have just entered the MSSC Humor Hall of Fame. You will be permanently placed in the archives. When I told President Leon what you had done, he said, 'Ann Allman did *that*? Well, I guess if it had to happen to anyone, I'm glad it happened to her, because at least she can take it.'"

Still no one would tell me anything. After lunch, I went back to my office, only to find a picture of a blue outhouse hanging on my door with notes coming out the roof, and the caption, "Powder Room Melodies" on it. No one would confess to it. Finally at the end of the day, one of our student helpers who had taken the test, said, "Ann, when you whispered to the proctor that you had to go to the bathroom, it broadcast to all three rooms. *The suspense was awful!*"

An hour later, I found out that one of our counselors thought it was so funny that he had gotten on the phone ten minutes after the test and called every counselor he knew in the four-state area. Then the visitors, cartoons, bad bathroom jokes, and hecklers poured in. A superintendent of schools from three hours away came calling. One evening after I got home from work, Jack asked, "How come I just heard your microphone story from my friend Rex, who heard it from a friend, who heard it from a waitress at a truck stop in Joplin?" He paused for a moment. "In all seriousness, I'll bet you haven't told me the whole story and that you broke wind three times before you turned the thing off."

At the following fall faculty meeting, the regular mike malfunctioned, and someone brought Dr. Leon the one I had used. He gazed at it for a moment, looked back at the control room, and asked in front of 269 faculty, "Do you want me to go to the bathroom to test it?" On another occasion, in front of the criminal justice auditorium, he sought me out, threw open his coat as if he were going to flash, and showed me that same mike attached to his belt.

One year later, the academic vice president sent me an anniversary card. For years afterwards, I heard students claim, that at the beginning of school, the story was being told to the whole criminal justice student body. Frequently in the women's restroom, an unidentified pair of legs would ask, "Have you turned your microphone off?"

When I applied for a second promotion, I tried to think of things I had done in the category of "community service." At the very end of my promotion folder, I tucked in "Powder Room Melodies."

If I were truly expecting to be promoted, I needed to get rid of my ABD (all but dissertation) title. Did I really want to do all that work? Looking back, I remembered that in 1977, after finishing my doctoral exams, a professor in charge of keeping me humble reminded me that once you get to the top of that mountain, you can see all the other mountains you haven't climbed. However, circumstances didn't allow me to write my dissertation, so I had resigned myself to a permanent ABD status.

Jack was able to finally finish his doctorate when he was forty-eight. Now at age fifty-five, I was poring over a huge stack of data I had gathered on my night classes. One of my older advisees, who loved to heckle me, walked in and said, "Well it looks like the good Lord takes care of crazy people, and you qualify. Are you going to do something with that mess?" He looked around my office for a moment and spied a broom in the corner. While he was on a roll, he asked, "Is that your second car?"

I wanted to do something, but was statistically brain dead. Fifteen stat books in the bookcase didn't change anything, for statistics had gone through me like a cup of coffee. I whined to myself about being out of the program for almost sixteen years. I knew the limit was ten. I really wanted to do this project. My thoughts wandered to Jack who hated statistics like I did. He hated it so much he had his basic stat book buried in half-inch plastic and made into a wall hanging. The inscription read, "Never to be opened in this life or the hereafter." The completed project weighed ten pounds.

Searching through some University of Missouri materials, I learned the current educational administration department head was a former professor of mine, as well as classmate and counselor. An inner voice urged me to call him right then. The answer came back. "You can come back *if......*"

I started making notes. The Graduate School needed an explanation about the almost sixteen years. Show and Tell couldn't have been worse. Back "taxes" had to be paid for some semesters I didn't attend. A hairy-looking test had to be passed on everything I had learned from 1969 to 1977 plus everything that had happened since 1977.

I had already had two advisors. One of them was dead, and the other was working on it. Educational Administration had to see if they could put together a new doctoral committee. There was only one person left from my original one, and he was about to retire and raise Banty chickens. Fortunately, four of the five members of the new committee they eventually formed knew me. My claim to fame for one of them was my high school senior year performance as the singing angel in the Christmas pageant. I'd take anything I could get.

A big worry was that most of my graduate work had been in educational administration, and now I was a counselor with a combination higher education and counseling topic. Even to get through a dissertation, I had to attend a class in Columbia in designing research. I dusted off the stat books and looked in the mirror at my almost totally white hair.

I was the same age as some of my friends who were retiring. Some of my body parts were already failing to come to work with me, including my memory. Once I forgot to look, and instead of grabbing the estrogen bottle, found myself groping around in the one labeled "Anderson Animal Hospital." I wondered how the dog liked the estrogen.

The day of the big comprehensive test arrived. I tried prayer. I found questions over elementary education for which I had never taken one course, so I pulled every test-wise trick out of the hat I knew. Statistics questions loomed, and I tried prayer again. At that point, I was eyeing the sign in the professor's office opposite the testing room, showing a beaten-up gladiator with the end of his sword eaten off. It said, "Some days the dragon wins."

Something must have worked, as the only section I fell down in was the junior high. So much had changed, and I had not kept up. They sent me home with materials to study for a separate test so I wouldn't have to re-do the course. I studied it with a passion. Time passed, and I finally asked my advisor if they were ever going to test me on it. He said, "Now we wouldn't want to do something like that this close to graduation, would we?"

Almost the same thing happened with higher education, since questions from there weren't on the test. I was to be re-tested, but instead, was asked what I thought I needed to learn. School law. The kindly Banty rooster guru smiled, and I bought the books he recommended.

After I had started the required class in January in designing research, the new professor in charge of keeping me humble found out the hard way I was not a woman of few words. Comments to his colleagues that leaked out were, "I tell my students to write too much instead of too little. I never should have said that to her!" Or "You'll never have any trouble working with Ann, but if you have any prescriptions that need changing, you'd better get on with it."

I finally made it to graduation. It had been almost twenty-three years since I had started that program, and only one other graduate had hair as white as mine. This time I had a husband who was proud of me, was emotionally on my side, and who had helped me get there. The tears of joy came only for a second, when I realized that parents no longer came to see their children graduate. It was the children who were out there yelling "Hi, Mom!" to their graduating parents. Our 30-year-olds were no exception, and their offspring were yelling "Hi, Grandma!" I wanted to hug them all, including my advisor, as I walked grinning across the stage.

I was also thankful my advisor knew up from down, as some of the other ones were placing doctoral hoods upside down on their advisees, so that the pointy ends stuck up their noses. Some of them even posed for pictures that way.

(Artist never confessed)

Chapter 19

NOTHING IN MY CONTRACT SAID I HAD TO……

There was nothing in my contract that said I had to keep away from some measure of horseplay to torment my colleagues. That was a genetic link never to be broken. One of my role models was a professor, who, on Halloween, would put on farm clothes, comb his hair funny, sometimes pull his shirt-tail out through his fly front, insert some crooked false teeth his dentist had made him, screw up his face, and go up and down the halls posing as someone else.

His first victim was the president, where he plopped himself in a chair opposite his desk, and with slurred speech and wandering eyes, asked him for a job. It took awhile, and when Dr. Leon finally figured out who it was, he tried to keep a straight face and took him to some of the other offices to see if they could help him.

Another year the professor targeted elevators. He would stand in the hall and wait for the elevator door to open. When someone came out, he would explain to them that if it weren't for the professors here, he wouldn't be what he was today. As long as he was on a roll and all dressed up for it, his students told me he carried out the role all day in his classes too.

That gave me the incentive to at least start getting ready for big zero birthdays. One of the department chairmen was soon to celebrate his fiftieth birthday and wasn't planning to be too thrilled about it. His secretary had already called me asking if I had any ideas for something to do to him. Among other things, they were planning to drape all of the departmental windows in black, but they needed more. I suggested someone buy a large quantity of prunes and a little toilet paper and see if someone could find a biohazardous waste receptacle to place alongside them.

I brought in my mother's wheelchair, careful not to wipe any slobbers off of it. I found a motion-sensitive small square box, with an eye looking out of it, that would go off and yell, "Excuse me – excuse me – would someone let me out of here?" when a person walked past it in the half-light. Before he could make full use of the wheelchair, the custodian swiped it and propelled himself down the hall toward the business office to pick up his paycheck.

Of course that started a string of big zero celebrations, none of them honorable. To celebrate Ed the librarian's sixtieth, his secretary sneaked into his office and draped his ratty- looking philodendron with toilet paper. Someone brought in a fifty-three gallon drum, and thanks to an idea from one of Ed's colleagues, I shamelessly made the asked-for monstrous sign for it that said, "Viagra – Industrial Strength."

As long as I was in cahoots with the library, and knowing Ed was willing to wreak some vengeance somewhere, we made plans to celebrate Charlie the librarian's fiftieth. Since Charlie was my car-pool buddy in the summer and my neighbor by two blocks the whole year, I pretty well had his number, so I proceeded to write his eulogy.

Ed had made plans to borrow a Grim Reaper's costume from his secretary and wear it while he read the eulogy. He had to beg me to make it in large print so he could read it through the netting in the face mask. That would have gone off without a hitch, had things not gotten all hot and steamy inside the face mask, and poor Ed could hardly get the words read for the perspiration falling into his eyes.

Charlie was taken by surprise, since he couldn't figure out where all the information in the eulogy was coming from, until something made him smell a rat about who the author was. After that, Charlie, who was known to be more than frugal, made a concerted effort to collect a tip from me and from anyone else for that matter, every time I came through the back library door before classes started. Once I gave him an Argentine peso coin, and later he complained that it wouldn't fit in the pop machine. When I told one of his student helpers that, she jokingly said, "Well, if you ever want some cheap entertainment, come on over. I'll drop a quarter in his toilet, and we can watch him go after it."

One year, Charlie decided to commute to Kansas City in pursuit of a second master's degree. To avoid driving the last miles home to Neosho, then back again to Joplin the next morning, he put a cot in his office and showered in the physical education building. Since Charlie was a bachelor, Ed decided he needed a woman to keep him company in his cot. So Ed went upstairs and carried down the legless biology model, whose liver was exposed and the top of whose cranium could be removed so you could see her brain. Sometime later, I asked Charlie how he liked his new woman.

"I would have liked her a whole lot, but her liver kept falling out," he said.

I figured Charlie might decide to get even with someone, so I gave him fair warning that if he ever tried anything, I would push our lawn mower over to his house and mow a word in his grass. The alternative would be to put a live mouse in his mailbox, but since I knew his mother went after the mail, that remained just a threat.

Since Charlie and I went to the same church at the time, he did make the mistake of parking his car right in front, where I was able to hook a souvenir raccoon tail over his antenna. It seems everyone saw it except him and his mother. As the two of them sped off to supper later that day, she asked what on earth was flopping outside the car.

Later the library staff found out I had a life-size replica of a monitor lizard, one of many I had bought on sale for the grandchildren when they were smaller. Our son David's wife, Jan, had put their son Dale's lizard in with some vines in front of the house. I happened to mention that their lizard had met with bad luck, when one of their dogs took offense to it and bit off its nose. Charlie thought mine might serve some useful purpose other than sitting high up on my office bookshelves so as to not frighten small children, so he asked if he could borrow it. He started out by planting it in the chair belonging to one of his female colleagues. After that got the desired results, one of the students carted it off to the women's restroom on the bottom floor. An older student wouldn't come out, thinking it was real. Next he put it on the downstairs dumbwaiter, along with some books and models going up to fourth floor, with intentions of spooking Ed's secretary. After some time elapsed and he didn't hear any screams, he called her to see if she'd gotten the delivery.

"Yeah, but I'm sending that lizard back, because he doesn't have a call number on him."

The lizard finally ended up in the downstairs book return, with his tail sticking out of the slot. A few minutes later, one of the student helpers suddenly decided she needed to go home.

Another time, I got a call from Billingsley Student Center asking if they could borrow him. I didn't ask. Later the English department wanted him before the night classes started, and I didn't ask them either. Finally the arts and sciences dean called down and said, "Do you know your lizard is up here?"

"Whoops, do I need to come get him?" I asked.

"I don't know," he replied. "He might not be through doing what he's supposed to be doing."

I went upstairs to find the secretary peeking out from the English computer lab, and the lizard poking his nose out of a door across the hall. It was obviously for the benefit of a custodian. Later when I went upstairs to get him, I was met by the evening shift custodian coming down the stairs. I smiled. "How did you like that lizard?"

He laughed. "They thought they could get me with it, but I've seen that old lizard before."

One of the building secretaries decided the lizard needed at least one more go at it. So she came to get it, this time with a black mouse in between its teeth, and nonchalantly swung it by its tail on her way back to the office while classes were changing. Right before I retired, I decided she should be the rightful owner. She placed it on the floor in front of her desk and festooned it with vines hanging from the edge. Most got a good laugh, but there was an occasional faculty member not blessed with our tendency toward foolishness, who had other thoughts.

One day when I was e-mailing Ed and reminiscing about some of the awful things we had done, he told me that one of his pranks on his secretary had backfired. On April Fool's Day, he had posed as their boss and had sent her a bogus letter congratulating her for her good work and offering her an extra three day vacation. Before he could tell her it was all a hoax, she went upstairs to see about it. She wasn't too happy when she came back, so she had fliers posted all over campus advertising Ed's well-kept 1966 Mustang convertible for five hundred dollars. I remembered that day, because when I walked in to go to work, some of the financial aid staff was doubled over laughing because Ed was being bombarded with phone calls. By the end of the day, I heard they were still calling him.

One day one of the administrators made the mistake of leaving for an extended trip and forgot to roll up his window on the driver's side when he left his locked car parked in front of the building. We were going to decorate the front seat with a bouquet of flowering weeds, but there had been a big drought, and all we could find was some sorry-looking grass. So I left a business size card on the front seat, with a picture of a cross-eyed guy clutching his throat and announcing, "While you were out, your septic tank overflowed and the contents are currently cruising the neighborhood." An administrator walked by at that moment and said, "Why don't you just throw a bucket of water on the front seat and tell him it rained?"

A bit before he retired, another one of the administrators decided he liked my national park and sunrise pictures hanging on our office walls and would sneak in before we got to work and trade them for some of his glassed-in Indian pictures. One of the counselors thought it might be funny to draw indescribable things on their faces with a washable marker. By morning, the faces would be all washed off, and by noon, they would be all decorated again.

This went on for some time, until one day admissions was getting a little worried that I hadn't noticed the disappearance of the Grand Canyon. Sure enough, there it was in their office inner sanctum.

So before my evening Return to Learn class, I made a handicapped women's restroom sign and taped it to the culprit's office door. I figured that wasn't enough, so I got into his office to make sure he knew I'd been there. Then, that Friday afternoon, I tightly sealed up the chicken bones left from my lunch and put them in his mailbox. Unfortunately, he didn't find them until Monday.

Soon another opportunity came to get even. The Red Cross had a money-making drive, where you could rent an extra-tame diapered goat for so much an hour and delivered with a chaperone. I took the goat and headed for this same fellow's office, but he'd gotten wind of it and had hidden in the mail room. No sense wasting good money, so I took the goat upstairs to another department. The chairman had stepped out for a moment and was more than curious when he returned, to find a goat looking at him from over the top of his desk, and a counselor and the goat's attendant crouched behind it. By the time it visited the physical education department and the dean of students, the goat had earned its money.

The decorator-of-Indian-portraits didn't get away unscathed either. Since I knew Spanish, and he didn't understand a word of it, one day while we were waiting to close down the office, on a whim, I sat down on the couch beside him, acted like I was making romantic passes at him, and crooned to him in Spanish.

As I ran my fingers through his hair, he thought I was telling him how beautiful it was, how his teeth were like pearls, and his eyes like shining diamonds. But in reality, I was telling him he had crocodile teeth, only one eye, and hair like that of a gorilla. My colleagues were none the wiser, so I was able to keep a straight face, until some gal in financial aid next to us who knew Spanish broke out into hysterical laughter.

It seemed that quite a number of male faculty, at one time or another, had to grow a beard in order to appear professorial. I got a call from the student center that the dean of students was growing one, and that I ought to come over and see it and say something. At first I acted like I didn't see anything and finally went up to him and said, "Oh honey – that makes you look so extinguished!"

One day someone alerted me to the antics of a young woman in town, posing as Myrtle, who did professional embarrassments. For a certain amount of money, you could get with her ahead of time to help prepare a script for her to use on the intended victim. Then a time and place would be set for her to show up publicly, her large frame covered with a blue bathrobe, curlers in her hair, and white gunk all over her face. She could put on a voice like a siren and would bring along her younger sister to follow behind her with a video camera.

We decided to target our secretary, Lynn, on her birthday when we took her out to a local restaurant. However, at the appointed time, Lynn had to use the bathroom. Here came Myrtle, but by then, the people in there were aware of what was up, and like a verse-speaking choir, said, "She's in the bathroom."

Lynn came out, laughing and red-faced, and after she got both barrels at the dinner table, Myrtle leaned over and kissed her, rubbing her pasty white cheek all over Lynn's face. None the wiser, Lynn walked through the restaurant that way. She didn't discover it until I saw her looking in the rear view window of the car she was riding in. Then I saw her lips move as she said, "Oh yuck!"

Another year we set Myrtle up for a man who was going to be leaving the business office for another job. He was full of mischief himself and gave Myrtle a run for her money, but didn't find out about the white all over his face until he was long gone down the hall. The business office told me later that they hadn't had that much fun in decades.

Then came the age contest. Several of us were born in 1938, and it got to be a thing as to who was the oldest. Nobody at the moment could find out for sure when Dr. Leon's birthday was, so Pat, the math professor, made a point of targeting me as the oldest and kept addressing my campus mail to "Chief Old Lady Counselor." He should have known better, as I was already heckling him for not replacing the broken-off cover over his gas tank, which was probably lying at home on his dresser. So one noon hour, I went downtown and bought a bunch of silk flowers, made a nosegay out of them, and stuck them in the space below his gas cap so everyone could see them. Then I called security to see if they would come over and give him a ticket for something. Actually the car Pat loved to drive the most was one with 400,000 miles on it. I kept harassing him about getting a new one, but he retorted, "At least it's not my primary car."

For a time, I got away with enrolling some of my older and unsuspecting male colleagues in Japanese I, cheerleading, aging and health, and dance and exercise classes, and then dropping them out of class when it was timely. However, after awhile it got a little old for them, and otherwise a nuisance for the business office, and I had to give it up.

People kept asking me what I was going to do after I retired. I told them I was going to write a memoir. That created a lot of smiles and a few chills down some spines, including those of some faculty. Of course I knew I would have to change most of the names to protect both the innocent and the guilty.

One semester I decided to start on the outline. By the time I realized I was into overkill, I decided to use it for a purpose. I was in the midst of teaching my latest Return to Learn students how to write a two page composition in order to take some of the fear out of their upcoming English classes. I turned loose of the thirteen page outline, printed on continuous feed computer paper, and let it snake out all over the floor in front of them, to see what they'd say.

"You obviously haven't limited your subject."

"That's enough for two books. You'd better cut that in half."

"Are you really going to tell *that*?"

"You've gotta be kidding!"

"If you're really gonna do that, you'd better read some more Erma Bombeck so you can get a handle on things." Obviously, I had met my objective of loosening them up enough to feel they could heckle the teacher and start having some fun in college.

Since I was getting older and a few brain cells were misfiring, I decided I'd better start taking some more notes and even further refine the planner I always carried with me. I needed to start teaching my students how to get organized and get myself on the ball as well, headed toward book-writing. A colleague had already reminded me that life was a series of small I.Q. tests, so I figured I could at least carry some of my brains around with me on paper, with the hopes that I didn't lose either the planner or any more gray matter. My worst fears were confirmed when security called me at eleven o'clock one evening with the announcement, "We just found your brains in the parking lot."

The planner turned out to be a great teaching tool, but it was amusing to watch the unplanned types trying to keep one. Sometimes I'd see pages sticking out past the zipper. Other times people would find pages on the campus lawn. On student carried around a planner full of blank pages, hoping I would think it was being used so that he could get an A.

I was grateful for some blank pages in my own when the day came for taking notes, and a drug enforcement officer came to talk to some of the student services staff about the problems of methamphetamines in Joplin. I started writing down some of the meth ingredients he had brought – camp fuel, muriatic acid! Once again I felt so ignorant. I started sniffing students as they walked by, remembering the days as an assistant principal when I learned that marijuana smelled like burning leaves. I had come to the point where I loved these students and my colleagues as if they were part of my family, and I didn't want anything happening to them.

The time would soon come for me to leave all that and retire. Already I was falling asleep at my computer almost on the dot of 2 p.m. so I could get a refreshing fifteen minute nap. I thought I was fooling everyone, until one of the student helpers told me he'd been in checking for drool. I knew then it was time for some renewal.

Fake monitor lizard

Chapter 20

FRIGHTENING THE NATIVES AND OTHER CREATURES

As much as I enjoyed my job, I was always ready for a vacation, especially if I could get behind the wheel and drive. However, most sane women my age choose not to take long driving trips alone. In fact, my friends in the church choir asked me if I weren't afraid to do this without someone going with me. I responded that on the contrary, any evildoer had better be scared of *me*. A woman colleague in the registrar's office had the same concern and suggested I ought to put a male blow-up doll in the front seat with me. I thought about that for a bit, but figured I would undoubtedly make a wrong move and accidentally stick him with a sharp pencil or something and he'd end up buzzing out the window. Besides, what would I do with him when I got to some motel - carry him in with me? Leave him out there to scare away all the good customers? What I didn't realize, until much later, was that older women traveling alone are often viewed by the public as possible con artists, robbers, child-snatchers, man-hunters, Alzheimer's victims, or even rapists. I didn't care. I did need that renewal and some stories to tell.

The first time, I flew to Denver, rented a car, found a motel, and parked under a huge tree, soon to be infested with starlings. By morning, the vehicle looked like it had the pox. I laughingly asked myself, "What bogeyman is going to risk mayhem to a white-haired woman driving a car with 150 bird droppings on it?" I hoped they wouldn't corrode much paint before I got to Salt Lake City. That trip was a snap.

I was sixty-three years old when the next chance came. I packed nicer clothes to make me look like I was in charge, was expected, and would be missed if I didn't show up. It was different this time. Eight days before I left, we buried our oldest son, John, and his oldest daughter, Kelly, who died in a terrible head-on collision in Kansas. My husband's brother was dying, and I prayed he would still be alive by the time I got back. It had been a year of deaths, and my huge grief needed a rest. Fearfully, Jack gave me his blessing to go, knowing this was my dream trip through the Rockies.

I meandered on to Durango, Colorado, eagerly awaiting my pre-arranged train ride on the Durango-Silverton. Not wanting dirty windows to mess up my perfect picture-taking possibilities, I had reserved my spot in an open train car refurbished with seats. Too late, I learned it was an old reconstituted cattle car. Soot was in my face, on the camera lens, on my clothes, in my teeth, and in my lungs. I lurched back and forth, trying to take pictures of weeds and mountains flying by. I remembered I could buy colored postcards for twenty-five cents. I put the camera away, reached for a tissue, and blew out a snootful of black cinders.

Later as I approached Utah's Capitol Reef, a huge totem pole grimaced at me from near a farmhouse, and I stopped to take its picture. I thought about enlarging it, making a wanted poster out of it, and strategically locating it on campus with a colleague's name under it. Once at Bryce Canyon, a chipmunk greeted me as I got out of the car. I was loaded with raisins and nuts. After the first mouthful, he ran his tickly nose up my arm in search for more. An oriental gentleman and two oriental ladies watched for a moment while I fed one chipmunk after another, but the two women soon took off for a safer distance. The gentleman studied me as if he wanted to participate, so I offered him a little box of raisins to give to the animals. When he gave me a weird look, I suddenly realized that he probably thought I was offering him animal food to eat himself. Not knowing what else to do, I smiled courteously, bowed slightly and backed away, stumbling over a pine cone.

I visited my aunt and uncle in Salt Lake once more, thinking how nice it would be to live there. I wandered down their street and came upon a tombstone nestled among someone's front yard flowers that read, "Here lies the last dog who pooped in this yard." Then I was bound for Idaho. Pictures I'd seen of the Sawtooth Mountains didn't begin to reveal their beauty. Giant dragon's teeth protruded above me, making me wonder what geological event had caused such a spectacular scene. Before I left Missouri, Jack had worried about my accommodations in Challis. They were not a part of the motel chain I was staying in, plus Challis was a small town, seemingly lost up in the mountains. Wonderful, friendly people had done their best to refurbish this old motel. What did it matter if the carpet lacked a mat underneath and the toilet seat had character? It was the bedspread that worried me. The two holes in it, only an inch apart at the head of the bed, raised questions. Cigarette burns? Bullet holes? Where were the brown edges or the powder burns? I double-bolted the door and went to bed.

I had made plans ad nauseum for my grand entry into Canada. I had every conceivable document plus car insurance papers that took a month to get. I had eaten the oranges and the carrots. My intestines were growling from eating the rest of the raisins. I was prepared for any question, including my age and the true color of my hair. How could they ask – what woman would dye her hair white? I had used perfume and deodorant and carried nothing alcoholic. I quivered slightly, but triumphantly, as I pulled up to the station at the border. *All he asked me was where I was going and if I had anything alcoholic!*

"But I have insurance papers and all kinds of things to show you!" I cried. He turned white, then red, and quickly waved me off. A deer standing in the middle of the highway looked at me quizzically. I showed him my insurance papers.

The area around Banff, Alberta, was paradise to me. I knew my way around Banff from a previous trip, but I continued to get lost in

Canmore where I was staying. I managed to buy groceries and spent the next two hours behind the steering wheel sporting a hunted look because I couldn't find my way back to the motel. I was starved. I was ready to go back to the only grocery store I could remember, ask them for a live chicken, and eat it on the curb.

However, I knew the road to Calgary. When we took our Rocky Mountaineer train trip, Jack had that medical episode that put him in an ambulance headed for Calgary's Foothills Hospital. Once I passed the hospital, I felt I was safe, but soon I sensed I wasn't heading for the highway I wanted. I had a choice of stopping at a farmhouse or at a place where they made sewer pipes. A well-dressed, well-spoken sewer gentleman barely got me back on track, and I followed my nose until I could find my regular route. I left Canada and headed for Waterton Park.

In town, beasts with horns were grazing and lounging in people's front yards and roaming the downtown streets. Some gave me that "You're not from here, are you?" look, and others showed me their rear ends when I pointed the camera at them. I stumbled into a picnic area full of Columbian ground squirrels. Much like prairie dogs, they had their sentries posted. I made sure one saw me drop a handful of raisins close by. After one found them, I slowly drove around, slyly dropping raisins out of the car window. In minutes, the whole colony was alerted that Raisin Lady was on the loose. The landscape was squeaking in anticipation, and almost every hole had a resident standing at attention, waiting.

My next motel destination was Browning, Montana. This was another worry about accommodations. My fears were confirmed when six motorcycles pulled in with me. Oh great, I thought - a night with the Hell's Angels. I really shouldn't have worried. A long-haired man in his thirties cheerfully greeted me at the desk. I eyed his plethora of tattoos, one meant to conceal a long scar on his cheek. I was obviously overdressed. He yelled to his wife, who was in an inner room. "Ann Allman's here!" She came out and cordially greeted me. Perhaps my welcome reception was because no one had ever made a reservation there three months in advance. Or perhaps, as I glanced at the night's roster, it was because I was the only one who had paid.

The man announced. "I want you to know that everything in your room really works."

"Really? Faucets, toilets, everything? I asked, smiling kindly.

"Just wait. You'll see."

The next morning, the only restaurant I could find was in the shape of a tee pee. It was closed. Finally I found a hole-in-the-wall eatery, where a friendly waitress with dirty fingernails and missing half her teeth brought me a delicious breakfast. In between customers, she sat in a corner and smoked. Three men sat in the booth next to mine, making intelligent conversation about the business of running their local college. I wanted to join in, but couldn't spare the time.

I really wanted to go back home via Colorado and revisit Estes Park, but I was running too late. The first time I saw it, I was an eighteen-year-old attending a church camp, and it was there I met Jack Hamilton. He was chumming around with a couple of fellows I knew, who decided to ask me if I'd like to go up to the lake and look around. It was a beautiful view, but somehow I was distracted by a dead fish floating on its side, with a hook and part of a line still in its mouth. I could tell it hadn't been dead very long, so I snatched it up, figuring something in that good a shape shouldn't go to waste. The boys started up a chorus about how I wasn't going to put that thing in their car, until they finally gave in and let me hang it out the window as we rode back down the mountain.

My roommates weren't the kind to keep curfews, so I knew I had plenty of time to do something with it before they staggered in way after dark. Around 10 p.m. I gently laid it in the water inside the toilet, where it rolled over on its side, giving me a fixed stare with its one good eye. I tied the line to the bar at the back of the stool and went to bed.

Two years after my big Rocky Mountain trip and right before I retired, I headed west again. After leaving my motel in Vega, Texas, where a prisoner transport truck had been parked all night, I headed for Reno. On the way, I stopped at the outskirts of Wendover to chip up some souvenir globs of salt for the staff at school. I could imagine comments of passers-by as they sped down the highway, seeing some old coot out there with her white hair and frilly blouse. With the exception of a train stop through it, I hadn't been to Reno since 1958. The old sign by the tracks that said "Reno – The Biggest Little City in the World" was gone, and had been relocated close to the police station. The flashy new one should have scared the trains off their tracks.

I stayed at the home of an old family friend, who guided me to our old forties home plus the building that housed the pickled pelicans and Father's office. Then we went to Idlewild Park to see the multiple generations away from the ducks there that I used to feed. As we swung back toward campus, I noticed our neighborhood grocery store had been converted into a pub. I thought about Father, who would turn down the TV every time a beer commercial came on, and wondered if he were up in heaven sizzling about it.

I obviously hadn't wiped all the manure off my feet before trying to dodge 10 lanes of Interstate traffic going in and out of Sacramento, headed for a reunion with Mother's cousins. Mother's cousin Bill took me to Sutter's Fort, where the lady taking tickets mistook me for his wife (I was in my sixties, and he was in his eighties.) He quickly set the record straight, but not without some amusement after we got home. We pondered over the number of men and women running around together claiming to be cousins, and felt the lady was thinking, "Yeah, – I'll bet."

By the time I got to Oregon, I had fingered every type of gas pump imaginable and pretended I knew what I was doing. After pumping the last of expensive California fuel, I coasted into the nearest gas station across the state line, only to be frightened by a six-foot-six giant knocking on my window. Seeing I was hesitant to get out, he announced that I was in Oregon now, where people waited on you. Too good to be true, I hunted for a restroom, only to see something less than a his-and-her Porta-Potty nestled against a bluff. I passed and waited for a restaurant.

Some hours later, I met my cousin, Mac, and his family in Olympia. I hadn't seen him since we were kids and had never met his wife, Susan, and their two children, Stephanie and Sheridan. After way too much merriment over what had happened in that fifty year lapse, Stephanie courteously came to the upstairs railing the second night to remind us it was four in the morning. A day later, Mac and I headed for a tour of the Olympic Peninsula. I'm afraid I embarrassed him by consenting to the use of a Honey Bucket at a questionable gas station with no air conditioning, tended by a sweaty attendant oblivious to deodorant.

Then I was off to Blaine, Washington. Almost the same amount of time had elapsed since I'd seen my classmate Bill, who last saw me with a matchstick figure, dark hair, and partially crooked teeth. The Internet had connected us and filled in a lot of gaps, allowing him and Darleen more time to show me snatches of northwest Washington and a piece of Canada.

Crater Lake on the way home was magnificent. It was a beautiful, dark blue-sky day that my camera couldn't do justice to, due to the midday sun. When I got to the top, I wondered what I was getting into, when a kindly-looking elderly lady approached me, asking if I were truly from Missouri and traveling alone. My antenna went up. She had only come to tell me that she and her husband had been following me up the mountain and that they had marveled how I had reminded them of her one-hundred-year-old mother. I wondered where this was going next. Her mother, when she turned eight-eight, was still traveling alone, running here and there and enjoying the scenery. When she got tired, she stopped at rest stops, where she slept in her car for the night. Once a highway patrolman tapped on her car window to ask if she were okay and if she wouldn't prefer to go to a motel. She thanked him and said she was fine. So he patrolled some extra times that night.

Luckily her daughter only wanted to compliment me for my courage in doing what I was doing and to wish me well. I started for home, thinking about my own parents and what their last days were like.

John Allman

Chapter 21

FRENCH-KISSING IN THE NURSING HOME, SHUCKING BODY PARTS, AND MORE PETS

I hadn't realized it, but my parents had always wanted to come to the Lenoir retirement complex sometime after they retired. My working there as a teenager had set the stage. Luckily for them, it opened up and accepted a wider population than just full time Christian service workers. They sold their house and bought one of the cottages that had since been built, knowing they could move from there into the manor, where there was assisted living. Eventually they could go to the new health center when they became more incapacitated.

A few years later, Mother had to go to the health center temporarily to recover from hip surgery, and as Jack, Father, and I were leaving from a visit, Jack noticed their names on a plaque listing donors for those who needed financial assistance to be able to live there. Jack said, "Edward, I notice your and Elizabeth's names up there as good givers."

Father looked up at their names for a moment and kept on walking, saying, "Oh them. They're deadbeats."

Both Mother and Father ended up in the health center - Father with advanced Parkinson's, and Mother with some dementia and extreme difficulty getting around. Mother told me that Father, in spite of his shaking and not seeing well himself, had been trying to feed an old friend in the dining room, as his friend was going blind and having trouble manipulating his food. Soon afterwards Father was put in the Alzheimer's unit, since Parkinson's and Alzheimer's patients share some of the same symptoms. I asked if Father could have a phone so we could talk to him more often. The attendant said, "Well, we ordinarily would, but people in this unit try to call their lawyers and 911 and people you don't want to know about, so we had to quit that."

I never saw two older people live out their last days as cheerfully and uncomplaining as my two parents did. They were in separate units, but could wheelchair themselves in to see each other and could eat together. Only once did Mother not recognize Father and chased him out of the room in her wheelchair. Toward the last, Father was almost completely blind, and Mother was getting more and more forgetful. Once when Jack and Dennis and I came to see them, Dennis saw Father first and asked him where Grandma was.

"She's over there collecting her thoughts," Father said.

Mother wasn't the only one collecting things. One of the residents in the manor had a habit of bringing things out of his room and walking into someone else's looking for a trade. When no one was looking, he would trade his bedspread for someone's shoes or his hat for someone's nightgown. When the loudspeaker would go on, and we would hear there was an unwelcome guest in room-such-and-such, we knew to hold the door shut until they caught him.

Some things couldn't be squelched by old age either. An old gentleman started giving an old widow a special look, until she finally gave in and married him. They both lived on the same floor. So they could keep all their things, they kept both rooms, living in his by day and hers by night. When bedtime came, all the old tattletales would sit around getting ready to watch him leave for her room so they could say, "Look what he's doing, sneaking around again!"

After Mother died, we could tell Father was failing. To cheer him up, we brought him a sweet, almost full-grown sun conure that we had named Chiquita that had learned to French kiss. After we'd had the bird for three weeks, we brought her and a sizeable bird apartment to him for his birthday.

A crowd gathered in the lobby when we took Chiquita out and put her on someone's shoulder. As soon as the kissing started, everyone wanted a piece of the action. We had also brought a specially-made perch stuck onto a rolling stand that was the height of a wheelchair and angled across it, so those patients would have a chance to play with her too. That was great, until the bird started French kissing an old lady, part of whose breakfast was still in her mouth and quickly going into the bird's. After Father died four months after Mother did, we gave Chiquita to the health center. The last time we saw her, she was riding around on the pillow-case-protected shoulders of the laundry crew.

A few years before my parents died, I took over as their durable power of attorney and got a good whiff of what retirement might be like. I was already getting a little forgetful myself and had started misplacing things, starting with my car keys, which I eventually found in the freezer.

Now I had to find things of theirs that had been misplaced during the three moves it took them before they finally ended up at the Lenoir health center. The most urgent included the keys to their safety deposit boxes. We never could locate them, and finally had to call in a man to drill through the locks.

As he was doing so, he told the story of how he had done this another time, and the family was unaware that someone's ashes were in the box. When he slid it open, the large fan overhead swooped up the ashes and covered the people and the entire room and part of the bank. Father's box mostly had twenty dollar bills tucked everywhere, almost as if he had a love affair with them. I jokingly told this to one of the ladies taking care of him, forgetting his prudish ways, and he didn't think it was a bit funny.

Along with my parents' health issues, I had my own to worry about. I was diagnosed with macular degeneration, and was told that some day I would eventually lose my frontal vision. I took the vitamin supplement the optometrist suggested, read a lot, and loaded up on spinach. I learned whole wheat bread would be better for me, so I bought a wheat grinder and started looking for fifty pound bags of wheat so I could start baking my own. Of course I couldn't find any in adjoining Kansas, the wheat state, so I had to be content with finding a bag at a nearby health food store. It came with six weevils, which I studied for a few minutes, and then said what the heck, as I ground them up with the wheat.

More worrisome for the moment was the fact that I was sixty-one years old and my periods were still going strong. Where was the menopause I was promised? I talked to my doctor. He told me his mother was eighty-three years old and still having her periods.

"You jest!" I said.

"No. It's embarrassing for her. When all the other people are in Wal-Mart buying incontinent stuff, she's in there buying sanitary supplies."

Something was wrong with this picture. This was the man who was prescribing both her medications and mine. I trusted his judgment, but I asked around my office about who a good gynecologist might be and met with his nurse practitioner.

"Don't you think you're a little old to still be doing this?" she asked.

I ground my teeth and thought, "You're asking *me?*" They ran tests. I had fibroid tumors, one the size of a softball. No wonder I had started having two periods a month. During my pre-hysterectomy conference, I told the gynecologist my father had been a medical school professor. I did that with all the doctors, so they wouldn't give me explanations that were too simplistic.

That put him on a roll, and he proceeded to tell me that after he cut me down the middle, the first thing would be to gently lift out my bladder and lay it to one side. I remained unaffected by that because I was really only interested in whether or not I could take my uterus home in a jar. Or at least that softball. He assured me they didn't do that anymore. As far as I was concerned, they could rip the old thing out and throw it out the window to the wolves. I was telling my friend Norma about this, who had the same question about what her orthopedic surgeon was going to do with her shoulder bones after he replaced parts of them. After he gave her a really weird look, she assured him she wasn't going to make bookends out of them.

The second day in the hospital, as I was trying to walk down the hall, whom should I meet but one of my advisees who asked, "Why Mrs. Allman, what on earth are you doing here?"

"Well, I've just had a hysterectomy and said goodbye to my uterus, and my bladder feels like it's looking around for some lost furniture."

I could see I was in for no heavy lifting for awhile, which posed a problem, as Lady, our eighty pound Labrador retriever, was going to need baths, and I was in no mood to take her to the car wash. As much as I loved her, I yearned for a small lap dog. However, that made me think of that puppy stage again, and I wasn't anxious to go there.

After she passed the puppy stage, she became so lethally friendly, that Jim told us one day, after he walked into the house for a surprise visit, "Your dog let me in and showed me where the silverware was and then made me a cup of coffee."

We bought a new king-sized bed with a softer mattress so I wouldn't hurt myself while I was healing. It seemed twice as high as the old one, and Jack had to work hard to get onto it. He swore the height was going to give him a nosebleed. Jack could be pretty funny when all his batteries were working.

While I was off work, I worked some more on Jack's genealogy to see if there were any more lost relatives nearby. I pondered over all the children that his great-grandfather, Will T., had by two different wives. Then I looked more closely at the dates. It was obvious he wore out his first wife having too many children, since just as the last one popped out, she died. Right on target, the second wife had a baby less than two years later, and after she'd had a litter, she died. The third wife was no dummy and obviously had a "Come to Jesus" talk with him, as they were married for twenty years without a chick between them. They must have had the same kind of deal Jack and I did when we got married.

I wasn't quite well enough to go back to work full time yet, when Jack and I and our friend Loren decided we might try to get into a one-night-a-week computer class at Southern. I was a real low-life to think I could get us all in free on the sixty-plus program, as long as the class wasn't full. Nevertheless, we made it, parked in handicapped, and took the elevator upstairs.

Luckily all three of us had some level of computer experience, but we just needed upgrading. Most adults our age without it were scared to death of computers, figuring one would break if they did anything wrong, and had no clue as to where the button was to turn one on. The books that went with the course were nice, but I smuggled in some of my pertinent copies from the *Dummies* series. I already had a lot of those in my office bookshelves from prior years. One day a student walked in, and seeing them, asked, "I wondered what kind of people read those."

"Smart people," I said.

The professor happened to know all three of us, so we made it a point to cause trouble in class. That was always a good strategy to get the older students loosened up enough to ask questions. Most of the younger students already knew ten times more than we did anyway, and we could pair up with them for help if we needed it.

By the time I got back to work, my energies had shifted back to animals. One day I walked into the pet store to be surprised by a cage full of half-grown prairie dogs. I was intensely curious about prairie dogs as pets. The pet store had finally decided to keep one from an earlier litter, and later I had the opportunity to watch him grow up. He made friends with everyone and eventually was well-behaved enough to wander about the back of the store without doing some prairie dog art on the shelf legs. I found out they were notorious chewers and would reconfigure anything – drapes, carpets, backs of bookcases, chair legs or metal carpet sweepers.

About a year later, I walked into that same store, and there was a huge tub with about seventy-five eight-week-old prairie dogs in it. I called home and pleaded. With great hesitation, Jack said yes, and for the next hour I sat alongside the tub with my hand down in it to see which little one was going to bond with me. As with other pets, I wanted to eliminate the squabblers, overly shy, dependent, fraidy-cats, or sickly. The same little prairie dog companion kept coming back to me, so I bought him a cage and took him home.

Getting Sammie at that age was the right thing to do. Either he thought we were prairie dogs or he thought he was human, it was all the same. He wasn't afraid of us, but for some reason he was very suspicious of his food dish. He wouldn't make much noise, but if anyone sneezed, coughed, blew his nose, or passed gas, he would sound off like a ruptured goose, standing on his hind legs with his nose pointed to the ceiling. Even as a voracious eater, he would rather have his tummy or nose petted than eat, and when we would try to take away our hands to leave, he would hang on to them for dear life with all fours.

Later we bought him a prairie dog apartment equipped with a chinchilla-sized running wheel which kept him busy for hours. I let the parrot walk on top of Sammie's cage to see what he would do. The parrot looked at him for a moment with one eye cocked, called him with a dog whistle, and said, "Come 'ere."

That same pet store had a Mexican parrot that I had been curious about. He was obviously not welcomed by his former owners, who brought him to the store in the back of an old pickup truck. He was reputed to have been taught a series of swear words, which I really didn't believe, as I'd never heard a parrot swear. So I asked him about a bad word they said he knew.

"Is it true you know how to say it?

He shook his head no.

"Come on," I said. "I know you can do it."

He nodded his head up and down and recited it, with a nasal twang to it.

I had been warned about a parrot on the other side of the store who would try to sweet talk you into petting him and then would bite you when you got close enough. So I kept my distance and talked to him for about ten minutes. Unable to get at me, when I turned around to leave, he said, "Oh, well."

Rae was a twenty-year-old macaw, who had been kept as the store pet. She was currently up on the top shelf in the dog section throwing rawhide dog bones at customers. A parrot nearby was bobbing his head up and down and chanting, "Bad Rae, bad Rae!"

That reminded me of another parrot owned by a kindly, older couple. When the wife died and the man remarried, the new wife and the bird didn't get along. When he'd make ugly advances toward her, she'd come at him with a fly swatter. After that, if she got any closer than ten feet away, he'd scream, "Fly swatter! Fly swatter!"

I was telling bird stories to our veterinarian, Kent, one day, and he told me about a cat that had to be brought in with a leg so badly hurt that he had to amputate. However, the owner wanted the leg so she could bury it. Not knowing any of this, a vet assistant came in on a later shift, saw the cat, and said, "Good grief! What happened to this cat? She looks like she's already got one foot in the grave!"

Thinking one day we would like to have a baby skunk, I asked Kent if he were willing to de-fume one if we got it. When he assured me he didn't do skunks, I had to resign myself to getting out the picture I had taken of a wild, baby skunk acting like he was going to spray my camera and hung it over the toilet.

As I glanced from time to time at that little skunk and at the other pictures of our myriad of pets, I felt both sad and happy thinking about our loved ones who had died, and all the animals that had come into our lives and had gone all too quickly. After Mother and Father died, I kept wanting to thank them over and over again for raising a daughter not to be the type that screamed at mice while standing on a chair, but one who could pet a grass snake, hug a bird, or dance with a little prairie dog. These little animals had been our companions in life and in death, as we had been theirs. I secretly hoped that when my own last rays of life were fading, a little bird would be perched beside me, singing my way into heaven.

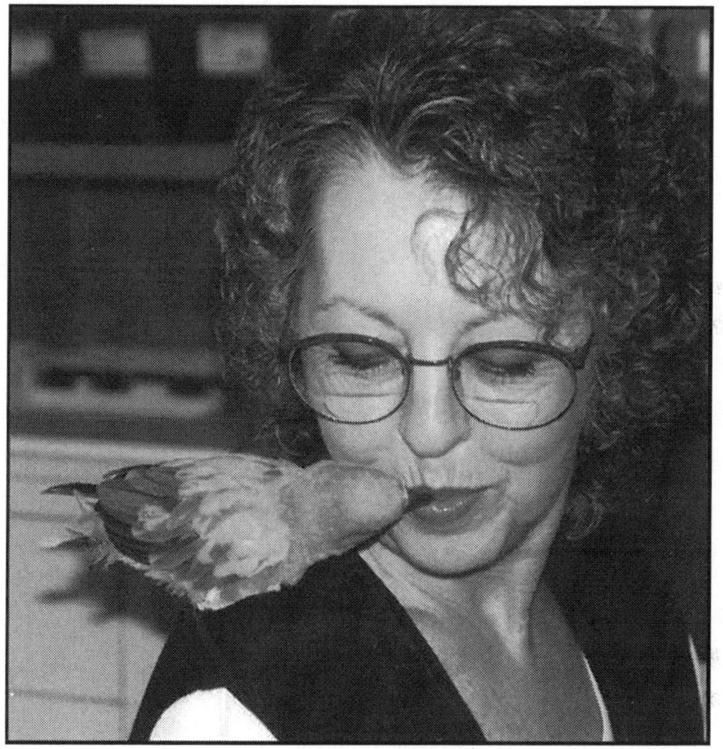

MSSC secretary, Lynn, and Chiquita

Chapter 22
SHE SMELLS LIKE MOTHBALLS

I wanted to cry. Medicare finally arrived, and it was time to pack up the office and go home, after fifteen wonderful years at Missouri Southern and forty years in the working world. There were so many good memories from Southern, and it was so hard to think about leaving it. But I knew I would be back from time to time. When I did wander back to visit the gang a few days later, something in the conversation led to looking and smelling better. Pointing to me, my colleague Erik said, "She smells like mothballs ....and formaldehyde." I knew I would have to get even with him.

I felt like I was at loose ends and was getting pretty worried about what I could do now that would make a difference in people's lives. I needed a purpose and something to focus on. I thought about the time I had asked Millie what she was going to do after she retired.

"I'm going to be a bum," she said.

That sounded like a plan. I tried it for a few days, but I wondered who was going to do all the things I didn't get done while I was working. Mice were leaving their calling cards on my parents' boxes still in storage in the shed after too many years. Spiders were hanging upside down in the corners laughing at me. I still had boxes of things I'd brought home from the office.

I finally started unpacking some of them, figuring if I didn't, we might start qualifying for the neighborhood slum award. Surely there would be more victims I could use my "Crime Scene" and "Hazardous

Materials" yellow tape on. Both had become part of the collection I had at home that already had a monster plastic rat in it like the one in our orthodontist's office. When I first saw that rat with braces on his two front teeth, I knew I had to have one. After I finally found it, his assistant offered to put on the braces.

I worked on the computer for awhile. Our youngest grandson, Kurt, had just become poster boy for a major brand of dog food and his face had recently appeared on the puppy trial size featured at a local store. That was another story. He had sent us an autographed empty dog food sack, so I thought I'd make him up his own poster that he could pass around to his friends. I wasn't really in the mood for spiders and mice just yet.

After awhile, I just needed to get out of the house and do girlie things. For the first time in a long while, I had spare time and could wander through stores checking out the inventory, instead of just snatching up items and throwing them in a cart. I sniffed fragrant body washes and looked for things that would make me appear younger, such as fancy spot remover for my face. I studied perfumes. I never knew so many nice fragrances could have such naughty and silly names. I realized that there would be more nice things when they started stocking up for Christmas. For now, the only things that were moving out were garden supplies. I noticed Baby Jesus nestled against the mosquito repellant for awhile before they got on with it.

I thought about getting someone to give me a permanent. I'd done it myself since I was twenty-three, and I needed my hair to look like something better than a furnace filter when I stood in the light. I found a beautician with a nice shop in her basement. On a table nearby, lay a small jug inscribed on the side with "Ashes of Old Lovers," which pretty well primed me for what the conversation was going to be all about. In the middle of all the permanent wave fumes, I thought about Dennis' right-hand man at work, and what he said after his secretary returned from getting her hair done.

"Gee, you were supposed to tease it, not scare it to death!"

You'd think I would have learned something from Jack who had retired thirteen years earlier. At first he decided to relax and watch some of his favorite class F westerns, but later I caught him watching programs involving snakes. That came as a complete surprise, as he had been deathly afraid of them most of his life. This was partly due to an unfortunate incident where he walked into a dark hallway and was accosted by some that had escaped from the biology lab. He knew I wasn't afraid of them or much of anything else, and had told me emphatically, "You put a snake in my face with that little forked tongue waving at me, and I'll be in Seneca in ten minutes dragging my hemorrhoids behind me!"

Pretty quickly, he got into something more constructive. For awhile he went to work for the Missouri School Boards Association and took to it well, but sometimes had trouble locating some of the small schools he needed to visit. He claimed he wasn't sure the American Indian had ever been to some of the places he was assigned to. People were reluctant anyway to give directions to a man in a suit and tie, fearing he might be the revenue man. Later he tried substitute teaching for awhile. I wondered how that was going to work, as he'd been a superintendent of schools for most of his career. When he came home after his first day, I asked him.

"Well, I killed three and stuffed two others in their lockers."

Finally he got a thing going at home. We both belonged to the Neosho Senior Citizen's Club, but the men's pinochle card gang had mostly died off, and those that were left came to play cards at our house. Before they left their rented building downtown, the men decided that the chairs in front of their playing spots were too hard on their bony butts and kept dropping hints for someone to make them some pillows. I decided I could do that, only on one of them I sewed a giant lifelike plastic horsefly. The men decided to pull a fast one on their master bug-killing marksman, John, so when he entered the room, they told him to stop right where he was and grab the flyswatter hanging next to him. John sneaked up on the fly and practically beat the pillow to death before he discovered he'd been had.

When there were only four men left, even one of those moved away. The remaining three, including Loren and John, thought it might be cute to advertise in the local paper for a fourth. One of its reporters heard about it and came over and wrote up a feature article with their pictures in it, which they wanted titled, "Three Grouchy Old Men Looking for a Fourth." That got around town pretty quickly, but they only got one call from a lady claiming her father would be interested. When they finally got ahold of him, they could tell he'd been roped into it, as he seemed to at least qualify for the grouchy part.

John finally got too feeble to play and had to move to assisted living. He did have enough energy left to torment unwanted boiler-room callers, asking the women if they'd like to go out on a date and trying to get the men to tell him what he should do with all the money they were offering him. When John finally died, Jewell, who worked at the pharmacy, offered to brush up on her pinochle playing and joined them. It took Jack and Loren awhile to get used to the thought of playing with a woman, but they gave in. Pretty soon, she brought in Pat, and after awhile they found Joann, the wife of that teacher in study hall who had gone after the boy making frog noises in the back row. Jack was a little concerned about what the neighbors might think about all of these women going in and out of the house, but Marvin next door said that at our age, they'd probably applaud.

The card gang never knew what to expect when they'd call Jack on the phone for something, as Caller ID would always give them away. He was already in the habit of answering "Yankee Stadium" when he knew who was on the other end. This eventually escalated to "Newton County Diaper Service" and some others not to be repeated, like Dennis's answer when he knew the call was coming from home.

Earlier, I figured I might as well be useful somewhere and ended up with the treasurer's job for the rest of the Senior Club members. The current one was 93 and had bladder cancer and really didn't feel up to it anymore. One thing led to another, and pretty soon I was also the secretary, because most of them didn't have enough computer skills to put out the yearly membership pamphlet. It was hard getting members, since age was taking its toll, plus some who could join were in denial that they were senior citizens.

The Presbyterian Church was more than gracious about letting us use their facility to have a pot luck supper once a month. Rich, its minister, was always asked to join us. He was single and didn't seem to object to a good meal. Soon he started bringing an attractive lady with him, and before long we discovered he'd proposed, so we started needling him.

"Rich, if you're the minister, who's going to marry you?"

"I am," he said.

With a straight face, a parishioner said, "We're going to have a pre-recorded service with a cardboard figure of him standing up there next to himself."

Trying not to smile, Rich said, "And to make matters worse, since the minister can't be a member of the church, and she's not one either, the church told me that we'd have to pay for the facility." A member did comment that someone at the courthouse assured them that a minister couldn't marry himself, which disappointed quite a few.

I thought about some of our other retired relatives. After he retired, one of Mother's cousins said about himself and his buddies down at the Elk's Club, "We're just a bunch of old men with skinny legs and big bellies and rears that look like Venetian blinds." Before we got to that stage, Jack and I realized we had better start doing some planning. Years ago, Jack and his brother, Doc, had purchased four adjoining cemetery lots in Anderson. Something led us to making sure all was in order, but in the process, we discovered some man had been buried in Jack's spot. Jack had already been concerned about a big tree alongside our graves that was growing all too close, and several times had commented on how on earth they were going to be able to slide him under it. Now things were really getting crowded.

The mis-burial was obviously a mistake, which posed a problem both for us and for the funeral home. Jack feared the deed to his lots had been lost in the divorce between him and Polly, but fortunately I had found it among his personal papers and had filed it away. Not wanting to upset the family of the dead gentleman, the funeral home tried to persuade us to accept two lots in another part of the cemetery. We thought a long time; however, Jack and Doc had owned those lots for over forty years, and Doc and Margaret had already been buried in theirs. The dead gentleman had to move out.

This wasn't our only property issue, as one involving my parents dragged on into our retirement. A few years back, I had gotten a phone call from a second cousin wondering why she had just received a mystery seven hundred fifty dollar check. When I found out the source, I realized it was her family's half of money paid not to farm some property in Bogard, MO, that her family and my family had inherited a long time ago. Unfortunately, my parents had been trying for 40 years to get rid of this particular life estate and hadn't succeeded. My cousin didn't have a copy of the deed or anything else for that matter. I did, but her family had looked after the property and its succession of sharecroppers over the years and had more first-hand information about it. We pooled our knowledge, and then the struggle began to get it sold.

That was a comedy of errors. First I had to prove in 1997 that my grandfather, born in 1873, was dead. Then there was a third party on the deed with no name. I had to find out who she was, plus whether or not she ever married, and if so, who her children were. Father had mentioned an aunt, and after going through countless old family letters, I not only found out about her and whom she married (the letters suggested a reasonably nice bum), plus the condition of her circulatory system, and how many chickens they had sold since the beginning of time. Only when I discovered paperwork from the Burlington Railroad, which bought a strip of the property to run the tracks through, did I find out who the children were. By scrutinizing the Social Security Death Index, I was able to kill most everyone off, thus eliminating any lurking heirs. Luckily, the second cousin was a real estate agent, and she was able to sell the property to an adjoining landowner who had called me earlier trying to get it at a good price.

Then she called me to ask what to do with the three ratty-looking cows that were on it. Considering their unworthiness for the market, we both decided that turning them loose wouldn't be the worst idea. I asked her how big Bogard, MO, was and if three stray cows would even get noticed. She said it was supposed to have at least a general store, but she didn't see it the last time she was there. It reminded me of a remark Johnny Carson made about a town being so small that it was located one mile past "Resume Speed."

Luckily, Father had gotten most of his parents' other problems resolved before he died, but one in particular had plagued him for months. One of his mother's insurance companies kept sending him a bill for her monthly payment, even though he had notified them of her death. Father's letters to them got hotter and hotter as months dragged on into half a year. Finally when they threatened to send the matter to a collection agency, Father became enraged and got out a large envelope. He pulled out his fattest red pen from the desk drawer and on the return address part, he wrote in huge letters:

EDITH LOWRANCE
LOT NUMBER 9824 (he made up that number)
SALT LAKE CITY CEMETERY
SALT LAKE CITY, UTAH

Like many older people, Jack and I found our calendar filling up with more and more doctor appointments. Once when we were waiting for Jack's Monday appointment at the VA clinic in Mt. Vernon, we overheard a gentleman say, "I had to sober up on Sunday so I could get here today."

Neither of us had experienced a colonoscopy, and Jack was the first to need one. The colonoscopy itself was painless, but drinking that gallon of gunk the day before was about as much fun for him as drinking crank case oil would have been for his father. By the time it got to be my turn, I'd set up all kinds of projects to keep my mind off of it. I learned the gallon of gunk wasn't half bad if you drank eight or ten ounces at a time instead of twelve or more, and that time passed quickly if you had something to do. I brought in a couple of books, supplies for a manicure and a pedicure, and washed my hair beforehand so I could fritter another hour away rolling it up. For those moments when it was safe, I cleaned out the cupboards and drawers in front of me, and before I knew it, that gallon jug of very cold liquid was empty. How I managed to get through all that, and then stab myself in the ear with a Q-tip five days later so that I bled for another four, I'll never know.

As for me, only once did I have to utter a bad word over a mammogram. After that it seemed that every time I went in for one, the technician was one of my former advisees. We started swapping stories about where women put their markers after it was over. One tech said they used to have a big-leafed potted plant in the exam room, and one day when they hauled it out, they found dozens of markers stuck to the underneath parts of the leaves. I confessed to forgetting about a couple of mine until I got to water aerobics back at the College. Just for the heck of it, I plastered them to a locker door, where they stayed until painters came two years later.

I blurted out another confession to my departmental colleagues when we all decided to have an early breakfast together before classes started. Someone asked me if my day were going OK. I said it would have started a lot better had I paid attention to what I was doing in the bathroom. Like an idiot, I had picked up the wrong tube and was brushing my teeth with one of my medications, wondering why my toothpaste suddenly had gotten so slimy.

Rat with braces

Chapter 23
FIRE AND ICE

One day in June, Dennis called to announce that his dad and Janet's trailer had burned up. The fire started in Janet's room, which was eventually completely consumed by flames. The smoke alarm woke Jack up, and when he saw his wife's room ablaze, he ran out the front door to find her. Someone said she was quietly sitting in one of their vehicles, smoking a cigarette. Having struggled with schizophrenia since she was eighteen, and later bipolar disorder, she was understandably making statements about aliens.

For three days, the Red Cross took over while the rest of us gathered forces. Janet had escaped in a tee shirt and shorts, with no glasses, no shoes, and no teeth. She did have her library card though. They both needed someplace to go. David owned a trailer park and had already told stories about some of his tenants and workers. He had one tenant with a house arrest bracelet on, and a worker living in another trailer whom he had almost given up on when it came to showing up. When it got cold and the worker couldn't afford the heat bill, much less food, he would do something to get himself in jail for just enough time to get through the worst times. In his younger days, David seemed to have a soft spot for down-and-outers, or else he figured he could hire them cheaply. He knew a fellow who would do almost any kind of work for him for a little cash and a six-pack of beer, but he finally had to let him go because he kept falling off the roofs they were fixing.

David put Jack and Janet in one of his rental park trailers and scurried to get it ready so the two could be in and out before Janet could get any more worried. Outside funding bought them a used trailer for their property, where David spent the rest of his spare time repairing it, installing things, and securing it against vermin and burglars. Janet asked him if he would make her end atomic-proof. We all pooled our extra furniture and supplies, at least enough to get them by for the moment.

A big problem still remained. How did one get rid of a burned-out trailer shell? David dragged it off to one side and got some orange paint and painted FREE MOBILE HOME on the side, along with his dad's cell phone number. After they finished laughing, David and Dennis both realized that it was futile, as their dad seldom answered his phone because he kept it in his truck.

The paint-on-the-side-of-the-trailer stunt was a bit like one planned by Dennis and his colleagues when they were working for a nearby agency. The best of them got together one day after Christmas to decide which salesman was the worst worthless jerk. They took out a half-page ad in the local free newspaper featuring a Christmas tree up one side and a fish across the top. The ad read. "We Buy Used Christmas Trees - $5.00 Each," and put the jerk's name and address at the bottom. Sure enough, trees piled up, and fishermen lined up, banging on his door for the money.

Two years later, one day before Janet's birthday, Jack Hamilton dropped dead in their trailer from a heart attack. Janet called the sheriff, who came out and found the family contacts he needed listed in Jack's wallet. Dennis was out of town at a special business meeting with his cell phone shut off. When he finally checked his messages, someone was frantically trying to tell him his father was dead.

"Oh no – which one?" he asked, when he called back. They didn't know.

Now came the question of practicality. The boys wanted to save every penny of Janet's money they could. They knew their father wanted to be cremated and for his ashes to be scattered over a favorite fishing spot where he and the boys used to go when the boys were children. That saved embalming costs. Next was the question of what to put his ashes in. They found out the funeral home would give them a free plastic box.

However, the funeral home was anxious to extend its services and make more money than that and persisted in its plea to also provide the service. After too much time had been wasted, David and Dennis bit their tongues and swore they would not say what they were thinking - "Just give us our Jack-in-the-Box and let us out of here." They left and planned a beautiful service themselves, staging it at a church where Dennis had once been a member. Dennis figured it was the right thing to do to at least upgrade the ashes container to his humidor.

Scott had flown in to join them, and the three decided to sneak off to the river the next morning and try to dispose of their father's 350 pound body and not destroy the environment. They hid behind trees as they scattered what was left of him into the mouths of curious trout.

When the river totally clouded up and began weaving like a blacksnake into the lake below, they said their farewells to Uncle Dad and took off.

A month before Jack Hamilton died, a fierce ice storm hit the same day that my husband had to be rushed to Joplin St. John's Medical Center by ambulance because of a strange pain in his chest. We knew the storm was coming, and with three pets at home, he strongly encouraged me to please drive back to Neosho while I still could while they were running tests. The week before, I had gone through arthroscopic knee surgery and was in no shape for a road emergency on icy roads.

This wasn't going to be like the ice storm of the early nineties where tiny beads of ice fell until the accumulation reached six inches. Then the ground looked like it was covered with deep snow; however, nothing stuck to the trees. It was so slippery, that when we let Lady out to go to the bathroom, we were afraid she was going to break a leg trying to get down the slope to her favorite spot. Just before she reached it, she had to do the big one. Much to the amusement of the neighbors, once it hit the ground, it steamed and hissed and started rolling down the embankment and in between her front legs before she could even finish. She kept looking behind her in total confusion, but things wouldn't stop coming.

This new ice storm was to be a record breaker, and Jack needed to be in the hospital in preparation for heart stents. While pretty nurses were running their fingers through his hair and feeding him hot food, I was home alone on a four-pronged cane, with phone service, but no electricity, a Yorkie, a prairie dog, and a tropical parrot. After finding out how toasty warm I could be staying in bed with diminishing indoor temperatures, I got out the parrot's little travel cage and put him and the dog under the covers with me. That was pretty cozy and quiet, until the parrot went into his mating routine and started singing raspy bird songs for accompaniment, and the dog started passing gas. The prairie dog was perfectly content to bury himself in his hay and warm bed, with a bedspread thrown over the top of his cage.

Our neighbor Fran seemed to be the only one brave enough to go outdoors and went after our mail, dressed in her fuzzy slippers, using a sponge mop for a walking stick. Neither one of us could figure out how the mail carrier could get through all that mess. Freda next door and some of the other women and I finally got together on the phone to compare notes on how many bird baths we'd been able to accomplish without freezing to death, and even decided in unison that itchy, crawly bras had to go. When it got down to 46 degrees inside the house, Dennis and family slid in from Nixa in their all-wheel drive, bringing some wood they swiped from David, a hard-to-find generator, a flu cleaning kit, and gasoline. Their sons, Boone and Cody, alternated nights staying with me, and Dennis and Anita ran back and forth between here and Nixa trying to take care of everybody. Between this and wonderful help from neighbors and church friends, plus enough food on hand, I made it just fine, even though the electricity had been out for five days. The last two days I was finally rescued by Herb and Barb at church, who took in me and all our pets to join them, plus two more dogs and a baby.

Jack, in his usual fashion, stirred up St. John's. While he was showering, a nurse asked him to peel off the last several sticky pads that had been hooked to the EKG machine. The last really painful one was giving him fits, and no amount of twisting and yanking could get it off. Finally he put on his glasses to discover he'd been trying to twist off his nipple. The nurse died laughing, but when he asked her to please not tell anybody, he knew it would be a lost cause. By the time I got to the hospital a few weeks later to have some tests of my own run, at least two other floors knew about it.

It was still too icy for me to drive or walk, plus I felt the house was too cool for Jack. So Jeff, who had been visiting in Joplin, took Jack to Dennis and Anita's house in Nixa until the electricity came on, and Loren and I could go get him. When we got home, we found our resident half-tame mother squirrel in a nest under our porch eaves, where she later had a second litter in the midst of more icy weather. Her worries were small compared to those of Neosho, now on its way to a massive cleanup that would take weeks.

After the ice storm, I had mega cabin fever. Should I take another trip in the spring in spite of a sore knee and a recuperating husband? I thought about our train trip from Vancouver to Banff, Alberta, where everyone had treated us like royalty. I tried to visualize again the old elk they spoke about that roamed around near Banff, with a rusty bicycle stuck in his antlers. Once, while the train was racing down the tracks, our hostesses yelled "Bear!" We looked out the window to see it was only a statue.

We'd already been to Alaska to visit Jack's cousin and had seen what a moose did to her fence when he tried to jump back out of the yard. Alaska. I thought about one of our retired arts and sciences deans who had written up a delightful saga about his and his wife's adventures there, including his description of the Poop Moose they found for sale. It was a movable, wooden moose fashioned so you could feed it gumdrops through the front end, and by lifting its tail, they would come out the back. I found where I could order some, and we bought three for the grandchildren for Christmas. Kurt wondered if he could stuff the gumdrops back into the end where they had just come out. He was only halfway successful, when David looked over and said, “Don’t try that on the kitty at home, son.”

My fiftieth high school reunion turned out to be my big trip. I was truly blessed to be a member of the Columbia Hickman High School graduating class of 1956. It was a remarkable class destined to keep its contacts, thanks to a dedicated and well-organized committee, some of whose members were still holding us together after fifty years. After our fiftieth reunion, I sat back and thought about what had happened to us over the years.

The hospital had held me hostage for our tenth reunion, as I was busy having a baby. By our twentieth, I noticed many of the men had recovered from near-terminal acne, had filled out, had lost some amount of hair, and had grown beards, causing me to take a second look trying to identify them. Name tags needed to be large. Most of the girls still had their figures and were pretty recognizable, although there always seemed to be a couple of extra beautiful ones we couldn’t figure out.

By the thirtieth, some of the men had cut their hair, and a few of both sexes had eaten too many bonbons. Almost all of the women suspiciously had hair the same color as when they had graduated. Pictures of grandchildren were beginning to fall out of wallets.

When the fortieth rolled around, I had gotten my teeth straightened, was practically the only woman flouting my mostly white hair, and was not recognized by any old boyfriends. I spied a fellow who we thought was one of the nicest boys in class, but we feared was a little slow. He had gotten a Ph.D. in engineering. I asked him where he was living. When he said Pennsylvania, I said, “Boy, you’ve sure come a long way.” He got out of sorts, thinking I meant from his slow days.

By the forty-fifth, I had gained two dress sizes, lost almost two inches in height, and tried to hide on the second row for the class picture. By the fiftieth, I had shed the pounds. At sixty-eight we were all just glad to be alive. Two came in wheelchairs, and forty-one had passed away. Janie, who could make her voice sound like a man's, had gotten on the phone and threatened mayhem to those whom we had not seen in fifty years. They smiled and said they came out of fear.

Some even came for two extra days to have a grade school reunion. We found we could still make Wayne blush. Bill sought out his senior prom date, Judy, to apologize. He remembered being inattentive and boring. Someone said, "Look, she's kissing him!"

I said, "I see you must have made up with Judy. Gee, you might have liked that a lot better fifty years ago!"

"I liked it just fine at age sixty-eight."

Barb's hair was still a beautiful red, thanks to her beautician. Her daughter had asked, "Mom, if our hair is gray and we come to your reunions, and yours is still red, what are people going to think?"

We stood under the flagpole, thinking about all the football games where we had tried to beat the Jefferson City Jays. We were the Kewpies and proud of it. Carolyn commented that our football players sure had to be brave to wear a naked baby on their chests. Who thought of that name anyway? Why weren't we the Rattlesnakes, the Dragons, or the Fangs? Herb at church heard me commenting about that and said, "At least you weren't from UC Santa Cruz and part of the Fighting Banana Slugs."

Our tour guides took us to the old auditorium. I looked around and couldn't stop the tears. The sextet, the chorus and the orchestra. The woodwind quintet and all the solos, often competing for prizes. The assemblies, and the one time I came down the stairs from the senior balcony, dressed in my green formal, to join the St. Patrick's Day queen as one of her attendants. The Christmas pageant, where I was chosen to be the singing angel for that year. How I wished I could sing those high notes again and do "O Holy Night" just one more time for them.

Our school of 600 had grown to 2,100 students, and they were doing things with the curriculum that we never dreamed of. Yet we weren't running behind in those days. We got through two thick Spanish books in two years, and no one even thought about watering down the curriculum. We rose to the standards with no excuses, and the teachers made it fun.

We got onto our computers after the reunion was over and started it all up again, this time with more e-mails. Our faces were older, but our hearts were still young, and there was so much more to do with one another and to say.

After the reunion, I had to start making some more decisions about what to do with my knee that had taken quite a beating from the ice storm The other knee had taken one too, in its effort to do most of the work, but I figured if I took care of it, things might start looking up. When I finally could get in to see the same orthopedic surgeon who had replaced Jack's hip, he assured me my right knee wasn't going to get any better. After some thought, I realized I would be much better off experiencing some short-term pain getting well than some long-term pain getting worse. This time I decided to be better prepared and started looking over our handicap aids.

Much earlier, we had inherited a four-pronged cane from Jack's stepmother, Oleta, but spiders had climbed into the shaft, made webs, and had offspring. A walker had been given to us by Jack's brother, who had fixed it up for his wife during her last days. In spite of his effort to make it more comfortable, the handles hurt my hands when I tried to use it during the ice storm, so I had gone to the pharmacy for inspiration. I found some padded slip-up-the arm elbow pads which I folded over and attached to the handles with ribbons. The next day, when I was using it to get back to the pharmacy, a man who looked like he was in between genders was giving it fishy looks. I also couldn't figure out why some of the clerks were trying not to laugh, until I took a second look. Sure enough, the handles looked like sanitary supplies wrapped up in underpants. That did it. We bought a new walker with a fold-down seat. I handed the clerk a check and asked, "Would you like a mug shot and some fingerprints to go with that?"

Surgery was scheduled for the day before Halloween, the day that would usher my body into the bionic age. Thanks to the surgeon's advanced techniques, I was up and walking a short distance the next day and driving three weeks later. Not sure how I might get through an airport inspection with a man-made joint, I was warned by a friend, that just because I carried a card showing my total knee replacement, airport inspectors would still be merciless as to where they stuck their wands.

After my knee had healed to a satisfactory level, it was time to quit procrastinating over getting some hearing aids. I was realizing how words with similar consonant sounds were getting garbled up and a few things on the sports channels weren't sounding so nice. So I sent an e-mail around to some of my friends that said, "I think I need to get hearing aids and am doing some inquiring around to see who among my buddies wears them or knows someone who does. Also, where they go to get them, as well as get their hearing checked. As to tinnitus, I get that occasionally and try not to mistake it for tornado sirens. At least I don't want to be like my mother who kept leaving her hearing aids in her purse and in her underwear drawer and then griped at Father for mumbling."

One response from a colleague read, "I usually only wear the aids in class. I don't have too much trouble with regular conversation, and not wearing them also helps me ignore my wife more effectively. I do have trouble with questions in the classroom, especially from little girls in the back row who mummmble. I know another person who has hearing aids. I don't know where he got his, probably from some guy on the street corner who was peddling them, along with purloined wrist watches, from inside his trench coat."

Unfortunately, it was still too early for hearing aids. If I wanted to get rid of the awful words I was hearing on sports TV, I'd have to change channels and watch golf.

Scott

David

Dennis

Sammie

Baby

Chapter 24

WHO WILL CARRY THE TORCH AND NOT SET THE PLACE ON FIRE?

While my knee was healing, I had some more time to think about what my life had been all about and what I would do next. I had experienced a strangely wonderful career and even some joys in retirement. However, as time dragged on, I knew I still needed more of a substantial purpose other than that of animal caregiver.

Even at that, it was nice to have folks over so we could watch the looks on people's faces who had never seen a prairie dog or a parrot up close. They didn't know that a parrot could hold onto food with his foot and use it to shovel the food into his mouth as if it were a hand. Because of a broken but healed wing bone, twenty-three year old Baby was now mostly confined to his cage so he wouldn't hurt himself further. During his days of more freedom, he would sit on top of his cage and yell, "Help! Help! Mama, come 'ere!" when he heard the garage door open and my car pull in. Now he was down to dog-whistling for the dog and then meowing at him. Or he'd say, "Whoa, Mama!" when Jack and I were smooching in the kitchen. I'm sure he missed climbing the drapes behind his cage and playing laughing hyena when he got to the curtain rods.

Those old drapes had to go anyway, as Sammie had gotten loose one day and made a meal out of one of them, not to mention the printer cord he had for dessert. He had decided he didn't like his metal food dish and had started using it for a bongo drum; then began backing into it and digging up the air with his hind feet like he was going to China. His marathon races in his running wheel had slowed down some, but his voice hadn't. He was still able to alert all the prairie dogs in our four-state area for ten solid minutes, when he spied the hired window washer standing on a ladder outside and flopping rags at him.

After watching all the animal antics, I started wondering how many of our children would carry the genetic torch for foolishness and mischievous terms of endearment. Would the grandchildren then? Things weren't looking too promising yet. In fact, the grandsons had hardly reached the place of their fathers and grandfather, who had kept up the tradition of helping clean up after the women fixed a big meal. I knew that peak was nowhere in sight when I heard Jeff ask one of his nephews, "Are you wiping dishes or just standing there breathing?" Eventually they cheerfully got into the act with the dishes, but weren't anxious to get animal-bite tattoos.

One morning I got a surprise phone call from Marla, the chairman of the elders at church. She wanted to know if I would be willing to become an elder. Me? A woman who had stood on toilets, chased after students, been part of lizard conspiracies and drug raids, and who wrote live people's eulogies? Now they wanted me to visit the sick, serve Communion, act respectable at church board meetings, and look pious. What were they thinking? I had been so busy sitting in the choir loft, I hadn't even volunteered to be a deacon. I posed this dilemma to Marla's husband, Jerry, who was chairman of the board. He always felt it was his self-appointed duty to torment me during choir practice, so he said, "We don't want you because you've been a deacon; we want you because you're old." I remembered the comment a young preacher's wife had made, who found herself so deeply embroiled in church responsibilities, that she finally said, "The work of the Lord I love; it's church work I hate."

While I was trying to decide, my mind drifted backwards. I had been a part of this church off and on since 1961. I remembered the story a former minister told about the time, in one of his earlier ministries, when a skunk in his garage sprayed both him and the dog. He had to sit on one end of Fellowship Hall and the board members on the other. And the Sunday morning when the candle lighters got into a squabble, and a third child went out screaming.

I had watched a succession of choir directors, including myself and Robin. He could sing and play just about anything and could make the electric piano off to one side sound like something ranging from cathedral to honky-tonk Jesus music. Then Becky was hired and also became our teacher. Coleen from the junior choir days was hired to play the piano for us. You'd think she would have known better than to believe I had in any way reformed from the era of the silly songs. Both musicians made it a lot of fun for us. If Becky wasn't staging choir parties at her house for us, Jerry and Marla were. The latter worked away from their country home, so we assured them that if they didn't get off work so they could be there on time for us, we would let out all their pigs.

Although I had been a big part of this church at different times, I still felt I might be inadequate as an elder, so I made one last attempt to weasel out of the job. For the last few years it had been customary on Sunday mornings to announce birthdays and such, even at the risk of being struck dead for lying. In June, I decided to stand up and give them fair warning and said, "Well, folks, I just turned sixty-nine and I want you to know how absolutely lucky I feel. When my great-aunt was sixty-nine, she'd already been in the insane asylum for a few years." (A year later, I announced that by the time my grandmothers were my age, both had lost their minds.)

That didn't faze them. They still wanted me to be an elder, even after I had threatened to sign the guest book in the foyer as Minerva Fudpucker to see if anyone was checking it. Elders were supposed to act grown up. I thought about it for twenty-four hours and finally accepted. If they hadn't learned, after forty-six years, that the family torch for mischief hadn't blown out yet, they hadn't been paying attention. And if those in the church who had experienced me as an educator hadn't learned anything either, I figured they were brain dead.

Laughter. After all these years, life for most of our Christian family still kept up with our heritage of laughter, mischief, and love. Laughter was the stimulus, the balm, the connecting link, the healer, and the passage into the next life stage without fear. If you could laugh, especially at yourself, you could accomplish almost anything. It was all about watching Jeff call fish out from under the living room couch with Dave's Fish Caller. Smiling over David always wearing his plumbing clothes to funerals, except for the one time he borrowed a suit. Laughing over Dennis and his Christmas tree prank with his colleagues, and John eventually looking for a new wife on the Internet. Scott visualizing his mother eating a baby, and Jim wanting me to buy him some testicles at our Argentine butcher shop. Kurt with his picture on a dog food bag, and John's youngest daughter, Tracy, with her hands on her hips, shaming a snake that scared her sister during a trip through the woods. Based on our families' histories, we figured it wouldn't be too long before they all got into the act.

And what about all that career indecision I experienced along the way? Almost without my realizing it, it died a slow death and became transformed into a network of pathways for me to stumble onto soon after the day I heard a colleague say, "Parents don't care what hat you wear. They just want you to help their kid." I knew, even in retirement, there would be more paths to follow, more people to help, and more rocks and fallen leaves to overturn, to see if any shiny eyes might be looking back at me. I also hoped the Lord would continue to forgive me for a few things along the way.

I remember a lady psychologist speaking at a teacher's meeting who said. "Whatever you do, don't be dull. Put perfume on the sheets or pepper in the soup, but for heaven's sake, don't be dull." Maybe I should let the funeral home know ahead of time to leave one of my feet sticking out of the casket before they shut the lid.

Dennis and Lady

Boone and baby iguana

Made in the USA
Columbia, SC
19 May 2024